To the Staff, Clients & Parents of Paradigm,

 Thank you so much to the staff for all that you do & all the love and encouragement that you shower on every client. You are changing the lives of every client you help.

 To the clients, you are all so brave and with your lives just beginning, I hope you all open your minds & hearts to all that your parents & staff are offering to you. It is too bad that every person, whether or not they have large, small or no obvious challenges is not given a chance to explore themselves and better learn

Where Journeys Meet

The Voice of Women's Poetry

by
Catherine Ghosh
&
the Journey of the Heart Poets

Golden Dragonfly Press
2015

ways of communicating & living. Every day at Paradigm is a gift, eventhough you must work hard to gain as much is being offered to you. And to the parents who have made the hard decision to part with your child, rest assured that you made the right choice when you chose Paradigm. I hope some of you will gain inspiration from this book of poems! With love & gratitude, Laura
page 25

FIRST PRINT EDITION, July 2015
FIRST EBOOK EDITION, July 2015

Copyright © 2015 by Catherine Ghosh.
All rights reserved.

First published in the United States of America
by Golden Dragonfly Press, 2015.

No part of this document may be reproduced or transmitted
in any form or by any means, electronic or otherwise,
without prior written permission by the copyright owner.

To contact the publisher, please email;
goldendragonflypress@info.com

www.goldendragonflypress.com
1-413-437-0802

Cover art: Shailie Dubois
Back cover art: Shailie Dubois
Mandalas art: Julia Pankratova

Also by Catherine Ghosh
POETRY
Journey of the Heart: An Anthology of Spiritual Poetry by Women

We dedicate this book to all women everywhere,
and to the poetic voices within.
May your journeys of the heart and spirit
be laced with magic,
may your voices sing,
and may your stories be told.

"Start now. Start where you are. Start with fear. Start with pain. Start with doubt. Start with hands shaking. Start with voice trembling, but start. Start and don't stop. Start where you are, with what you have. Just… start."

Ijeoma Umebinyuo

Contents

Foreword by Tanya Lee Markul / xv
Introduction by Catherine Ghosh / xvii

Chapter 1: Voicing Heartaches / 1
Making Room by Jamie Burgess / 3
    Living by Breaking by Rosemerry Wahtola Trommer / 5
    Tears by Ruth Calder Murphy / 5
    I Was Not Alone by Heather Awad / 6
    Being Seen by Carolyn Riker / 7
    Maya by Taya Malakain / 8
    At Dusk by Alise Versella / 9
    The Pain of Love by Catherine Ghosh / 10
    Not Saved by Jenn Grosso / 12
    Wreckage by Tammy T. Stone / 12
    This Does Not Belong to You by Salyna Gracie / 13
    A Great Unknowing by Sally MacKinnon / 14
    The Vase by Krista Katrovas / 15
    Marooned by Ginny Brannan / 16

Chapter 2: Voicing Healing / 19
Healing as Transformation by Alice Maldonado Gallardo / 21
    Shamaness by Nirvani Teasley / 23
    Engulfed by Shailie Dubois / 23
    Rise Up! by Jesse James / 24
    Blue Green Compass by Laura Kutney / 25
    Grace by Camellia Stadts / 26
    Whole by Alise Versella / 27
    When You Think by Ulli Stanway / 28
    Unchained, Unbound, and Free by Jackie VanCampen / 29
    Mon Amie by Mariann Martland / 31
    Red Ribbon by Shailie Dubois / 31
    Letting Myself go by Ruth Calder Murphy / 32
    The Hungry Ghost by BethAnne Kapansky / 33
    For all the times... I thank you! by Sandra Allagapen / 36

Chapter 3: Voicing Shadows / 39
Dancing With Our Dark Sides by Anita Grace Brown / 41
    Listen by Ruth Calder Murphy / 44
    In The Winter of My Undoing by Sonja Marie Phillips- Hollie / 45
    From Inside the Tower by Kai Coggin / 46
    Impossibility by Ruth Calder Murphy / 47
    The Solitary Journey by Charu Agarwal / 48
    When I Feel Like I Am Falling From My Soul
      by Maureen Meshenberg / 49
    Sleepless Night by Mel Martin / 50
    Rhododendron Mile by Lisa Smith / 50
    Angels Above by Taruni Tan / 51
    Ghost Train by Julia W. Prentice / 52
    How I Bleed by Kathi Valeii / 53
    This Cynical Heart by Ginny Brannan / 55
    Everything is Dissolving by Gwen Potts / 56

Chapter 4: Voicing Light / 59
A Dawning Fullness by Ruth Calder Murphy / 61
    Radiate Love by Jamie Burgess / 63
    Ascendance of Light by Maureen Kwiat Meshenberg / 64
    Life That Knows by Helene Rose / 65
    Dancing the Dream Awake by MaRa LuaSa / 66
    Fireflies by Danielle Kreps / 67
    Planting Stars by Kai Coggin / 67
    Rainbows and Me by Charu Agarwal / 68
    Seek the Pearl by Sara Johansson / 69
    Pearls of the Sea by Carolyn Riker / 69
    Winged Prayer by Madhava Lata Dasi / 70
    Your Soul Holds the Flame by Maureen Kwiat Meshenberg / 71
    As the Movement of Moment by Jennifer Hillman / 72
    Keep Faith by Ruth Calder Murphy / 73

Chapter 5: Voicing Vulnerability / 75
Our Beautiful Transparency by Milijana Bozovic / 77
    Raw by Tracie Nichols / 79
    Of Things That Pass by Tammy T. Stone / 81
    Vessels by Shailie Dubois / 82
    Soul Scream by Catherine Ghosh / 83

Winter Sun by Lynda Vargas   / 84
  Tiny Boat by Kai Coggin   / 85
  The Ocean Within by Kim Buskala   / 86
  Of the Ebb and Flow by Ruth Calder Murphy   / 87
  In the Dark of Light by Tammy T. Stone   / 88
  Perfect Imperfections by Kim Buskala   / 89
  A Trusting Heart by Camellia Stadts   / 90
  Fear Is The Thing, My Dear by Charlotte Eriksson   / 91
  When a Woman Surrenders by Helene Averous   / 91

Chapter 6: Voicing Courage   / 93
The Water of our Soul's Garden by Carolyn Riker   / 95
  Strength in Being Seen by Victoria Erickson   / 97
  Why the Lotus Blooms by Charu Agarwal   / 97
  Night and Day by Alise Versella   / 99
  Fire by Jackie VanCampen   / 99
  Learning to Say No by Krista Katrovas   / 101
  Sky and Cage by BethAnne Kapansky   / 102
  I'm Not Afraid by Jackie VanCampen   / 102
  Flying into Nothingness by Alice Maldonado Gallardo   / 104
  Holding on to Letting Go by Darshana Mahtani   / 106
  Who Shushed your Shouts? by Anita Grace Brown   / 107
  I Can by Heather Awad   / 109
  Falling Softly by Romana Anna Nova   / 110
  SHE by MaRa LuaSa   / 111

Chapter 7: Voicing Soul Secrets   / 113
A Dance with Oneness by Tammy T. Stone   / 115
  Look Within by Jasmine Kang   / 117
  I AM by Jamie Burgess   / 118
  Sutra of Stars by Taya Malakian   / 118
  The Wind of the Soul by Nancy Carlson   / 119
  Upon the Riverbed of my Soul by Charu Agarwal   / 120
  Soul Song by Sandra Allagapen   / 121
  Alone Time by Krista Katrovas   / 122
  Flying Free by Charu Agarwal   / 123
  Silence, I am Yours by Vrinda Aguilera   / 124
  The Covenant Within by Sonja Marie Phillips-Hollie   / 124

  Reverence by Andreja Cepus / 125
  The Embrace: You and I by Zahra Akbarzadeh / 126
  Master of the Heart by Sitara Alaknanda Shakti / 126

Chapter 8: Voicing Revelations / 129
Searching for the One, the We, the All by Julie Prentice / 131
  A Stained Glass Heart by Carolyn Riker / 132
  Be Coming by Kai Coggin / 133
  The Season of Truth by Alice Maldonado Gallardo / 134
  Experience by Jasmine Kang / 135
  She Believed by Carolyn Riker / 137
  I am Free by Anjuu Kalhaan / 138
  The Things I've Built by Alise Versella / 138
  The Cheetah by Abra Duprea / 140
  Inner Mystery by Sonja Marie Phillips-Hollie / 141
  Words, Lovely Words by Louise Marcotte Desrosiers / 141
  Listening to My Inner Voice by Carolyn Riker / 142
  Awareness by Tracie Nichols / 143
  Meeting by Ruth Calder Murphy / 144

Chapter 9: Voicing Struggle / 147
Planting Our Staff by Tracie Nichols / 149
  Fence by Ruth Calder Murphy / 152
  Prisons by Sarah Courtney Dean / 153
  I forgot my name by Kai Coggin / 153
  Flower by Brigid Clare Oak / 155
  Lost November Days by Salyna Gracie / 156
  Heart Roar by Bryonie Wise / 157
  Exploding Sun by Gwen Potts / 158
  Disillusion by Dana Gornall / 160
  Breathing in Myself by Rachelle Smith Stokes / 161
  Sit with me in the I don't know by Anita Grace Brown / 162
  One Day by Yvonne Brewer / 164
  The Fierce One by Eva Xanthopolus / 166
  I Sip Solitude by Carolyn Riker / 167

Chapter 10: Voicing Prayers / 169
Heart Wishes by Sandra Allapagen / 171
  I Am by Shivana Sharma / 173

Praying by Ruth Calder Murphy   / 174
In Your Hands by Alice Maldonado Gallardo   / 174
Fraught with Peace by Anita Grace Brown   / 176
Leaning Into the Ether by Sally MacKinnon   / 177
Emergence by Tammy T. Stone   / 178
Bridge Between Hearts by Sandra Allagapen   / 179
A Poem without Words by Taya Malakrain   / 181
Faith by Vrinda Aguilera   / 182
Earth's Chapel by Nancy Carlson   / 183
Orion by Kai Coggin   / 184
Endless Flight by Milijana Bozovic   / 185
You and All Things by Brigid Clare Oak   / 185

Chapter 11: Voicing Motherhood   / 187
A Symphony of Bird Songs by Yvonne Brewer   / 189
Mothering by Ruth Calder Murphy   / 192
If I Could by Maureen Kwiat Meshenberg   / 193
Houses of the Holy by Jamie Burgess   / 194
The Child That She Could Not Bring Home
    by Yvonne Brewer   / 195
Creativity Reborn by Ulli Stanway   / 196
She Who is Exalted by Milijana Bozovic   / 197
My Angel in the Sky by Tanielle Childers   / 198
Valentine for a Vacant Womb by Kai Coggin   / 200
Living Between by Tracie Nichols   / 202
A Child is Born by Sandra Allagapen   / 203
Rejoice Old Mothers! by Jennifer Courtney Zechlin   / 204
Emptiness by Kadambari Kashyap   / 205
The Empty Nest by Charu Agarwal   / 205

Chapter 12: Voicing Love   / 209
And There is Love by Nancy Carlson   / 211
The Search by Darshana Mahtani   / 213
Heart Hugs by Krista Katrovas   / 213
Stone by Shailie Dubois   / 214
She Thanks the Universe for Loving Her
    by Laura Demelza Bozma   / 215
We are Love by Carolyn Riker   / 216

Love is All There Is by Ulli Stanway / 217
Back In Our Hearts by Krista Katrovas / 218
Opening To Love by Elizabeth Muccigrosso / 219
And We Would Be Free by Zoe Quiney / 221
If I Leave by Alice Maldonado Gallardo / 221
Enlightenment Catalyst by Jai Maa / 223
The Dance of Life and Love by Savitri Talahatu / 224
Shared Love by Jennieke Janaki / 225

Chapter 13: Voicing Our Sisterhood / 227
United by the Pages of Our Journey
 by Maureen Kwiat Meshenberg / 229
There Have Always Been Women's Hips
 by Dominique Youkhehpaz / 232
We Who Have Gathered by Maureen Kwiat Meshenberg / 235
A Message to My Sisters by Alise Versella / 236
I Honor You by Maureen Kwiat Meshenberg / 238
Sister by Marine L. Rot / 240
Old Friends by Ginny Brannan / 240
Golden Bauble by Anita Grace Brown / 241
Women's Tipi Time by Krista Katrovas / 242
Connections by Ruth Calder Murphy / 243
Star Sister by Krista Angelique Katrovas / 244
Abandoned Seeds by Kai Coggin / 246
The Dance That Bears Your Name by Carol Reedy Rogero / 250
She and I by Shailie Dubois / 251

About the Authors / 253
About the Artists / 265
Acknowledgments / 267

"When I need a power boost I sit in a circle with (mostly) women who also are trying to create a world in which everyone matters."

Gloria Steinem

Foreword

As women seek mentorship, nature, authentic expression, friendship, prayer, sisterhood, motherhood, lovers, creative projects and studentship, we begin to reveal ourselves in ways we never thought possible. We naturally turn toward our intuition and give breath and a voice to what we truly know. Not as one exceptional intuitive force, but as many hearts beating within the harmonious ebb and flow of life, and reflecting the She that is all around us and within us.

The She comes to us—as a beloved garden, a lit candle at dusk, during pregnancy, through a love relationship. The She comes to us—as a word, a summer breeze, a dancing tree, a story or a poem. The She comes to us—as mountains, as the heavens, as shelter, visible and invisible. She is the light and She is the darkness, and She reminds us of what we are made from and where our true home is. She is the journey and She is the destination.

There are no small or big roles to play. We are all the seeing eyes of an infinite sky and the nursing arms of a bold, courageous ocean holding onto the earth, both as wise one and as child. Each one of us arrives as an intricate part with a story to share, unfold, discover, create and reveal.

When we seek and offer the narratives of our inner landscapes, we create illuminated marks along an often-shadowed path—for ourselves and for others. In doing so we set an inner calling in motion—to assist us in discovering the many doors of experience leading us toward a freedom that can only be won naturally and on our own.

These personal stories translated through the art of poetry can be a turbine for inner growth, a vitamin for the heart, a circle for deep healing, a forest fire for rebirth or a storm for watering the seeds of your own blossoming.

Make them all your own. And perhaps let them inspire you to write your own secrets on the wall, to bear your own scars with courage; that you may be empowered by all of the experiences of your time.

The source of all of these words strung together is love—an unabashed, uninhibited, unashamed, warriorship of love. And they come from a work in progress called the human heart and they're meant to lead you back to your own.

Forgive and perhaps forget. Hold out for your tribe and walk in the direction of aliveness—even if that means something you never expected. Take your time and keep looking to the *real* that speaks to you from within. And, as the brave women in this book have done, come out; please come out wherever you are.

Tanya Lee Markul
Creator of ThugUnicorn.com & YogaWriteNow.org
Cofounder & Editor in Chief of Rebelle Society.com

Introduction

During times in our lives in which we poets feel as if no one is there for us, there is always the blank page. It captures the thoughts that toss and turn with us in bed at night, the feelings that squeeze our hearts the tightest, and the journeys we each take through our inner cosmos. Open and inviting, free from judgment and unsurpassable in its receptivity, the blank page inevitably becomes the reservoir of our soul's nakedness.

In contrast to blank pages that we fill in private is the often-critical public many of us sensitive poets shy away from. When it comes to sharing our writing, the world can often feel like a perfectionist arena of literary standards demanding proficiency, interested more in form than in substance. Intimidated by this, many of us keep our writing journeys to ourselves. Yet it has been my experience that writing need not be perfect to powerfully impact others. This is perhaps especially so with poetry, as even the poems of novices have the potential to have a positive and meaningful impact on the writing journey of others.

Nearly three years ago I began an online poetry project dedicated to creating a welcoming atmosphere in which women felt free to express themselves. As participation in the project began to grow, and hundreds of women from around the world came together to share their journeys, magic happened. Within the Journey of the Heart community timid voices gained confidence, insecurities dissolved, fears were cast aside and women inspired one another to just be themselves, unapologetically, uninhibitedly and most rewardingly. Through the process of writing and sharing poetry, a sisterhood was formed and this, our second volume of poems, emerged.

This collection represents the untethered voices and unguarded hearts of women who have been generous enough to share their journeys with others. Our journeys meet at the intersection of courage and trust where our stories finally start spilling out into the world, and moving the hearts of others in the process. You can't spot this location on a map or receive instructions on how to get there, for we each blaze our own trails in uniquely beautiful ways. Once having arrived, we realize that the path here is not formulaic, and that it doesn't follow predictable, straight lines from point A to point B. Instead, our journeys are dynamic, curving vortexes electrified by the thumping of our own hearts. In this sacred place our poems run in wonderful feral dashes through the wilderness of our lives, and the lives of others, leaving behind triumphant trails.

It is one thing to bare one's soul in private, but it is quite another to do so before others. While the composition of a poem is often accompanied by sighs of relief, the thought of sharing one's poetry with others can feel nauseating at times. Yet there is something deep within all of us that wants to be heard, seen and experienced by another person. We all long for intimate, meaningful connections with what dwells in our own core, the cores of others and of life itself.

The book you hold in your hand is the result of such connections. It is also your invitation to do the same: to experiment with the power of poetry to help you express yourself, in spite of yourself, and all your tendencies to hold back. To take a risk sharing your journey with others and feel exhilarated by it. For the voices of women have been held back long enough, and life longs to hear you sing!

May sisterhoods such as the one that birthed this book rise all around the world, to celebrate and honor the many valuable gifts of the heart and spirit found in the voices of women.

Catherine Ghosh
Creator and Chief Editor of the
Journey of the Heart Poetry Project

1
Voicing Heartaches

"Your heart expands when it's broken. A shattered heart mends but it has stretched. The stretching creates room for even more love. In fact, the loveliest people are the ones who've been burnt and broken and torn at the seams, yet still send their open hearts into the world to mend with love again and again, and again."
Victoria Erickson

Making Room

by Jamie Burgess

Our stories are powerful—the ones we share with others and the ones we bear witness to: extremely potent medicine. They break through our illusions of separateness and help us to make sense of the world around us. They hold the keys to our healing. One of my favorite authors, Sue Monk Kidd, once wrote, "In a way humans are not made of skin and bone as much as we are made of stories," and I see so much truth in that. There are times in our lives when we need to look back in order to understand what lies ahead of us. There are also times we must look ahead in order to get perspective on what's already passed. Most importantly, though, is learning to sit with the discomfort of where we are and allowing space for it. Not pulling back or pushing ahead, just being completely present. This is the space where our truest power resides, the birthplace of clarity and healing.

Heartache is one of the most painful situations to sit with, and also an inevitable part of being human. When we open our hearts to experience love, we also open ourselves to disappointment, loss, and fear. We cannot escape this no matter how hard we try because love requires vulnerability. It hurts to feel rejected and abandoned by the people we love. The feeling of hopelessness those experiences stir up in us is intense. Yet in those moments is where we find our greatest potential for growth. When we are feeling surrounded by darkness and desperate for light, we are forced to reach. We know if we don't stretch, we perish. So we find ourselves stretching, each and every time, no matter the distance required—and in doing so, we grow.

As trite as it may seem, deep in our bones we all know that a broken heart means an open heart. It is proof that something has mattered. It means that we have exposed our heart to another human being and taken a risk. We have chosen love. Knowing this truth doesn't make the heartache any less painful, but it does make it a little easier to bear.

It also helps to surround ourselves with other human beings, people who will hold space for us as we process and move towards healing. We need people in our lives to share our stories with. Their love and support will help pull us through. They will help us to remember that we are not alone; that someone else has wrestled with the hard things and made it out okay and that we, too, will survive. Shared experience is the glue that binds us all together. It nourishes us and makes us stronger.

Our collective stories create the human experience, and yet, we are only a small part of the picture. There is so much more at work here. The whole of the Universe is coursing along with all its various ebbs and flows and we are simply along for the ride. This is it… life in all its wondrous glory. The most beautiful thing we can do while we're here is to learn to embrace it—the love and the fear, the joy and the sorrow, the coming together and the unfolding—making room in our hearts for it all.

Living by Breaking
by Rosemerry Wahtola Trommer

Like any other muscle,
the heart, when injured,
will clench, and will stay that way

for a long, long time, most likely
long past the time of usefulness.
But when it relaxes again,

perhaps because it has been touched
in just the right way, or perhaps
just because it is exhausted

with its own clenching, well then
it is like when the sun hits the forest
in late morning and releases the scent

of pine and greening leaves.
And it is like when you walk past a spring
and a dozen blue butterflies all brush

you with their wings, a feeling so impossibly
soft and tender that you cannot help
but let the heart stay open, though you know

it will be wounded again. It is not
in the end the heart itself that matters.
It is the practice of releasing again, again.

Tears
by Ruth Calder Murphy

Rain—
Clear as wishes,
dear as phantom kisses

falling light and bright to the basin
of my soul.
Rain on the skylight of my third eye,
shedding tears,
not knowing why—
falling like criminals on gallows,
giving up the chance to dry
in favor of flowing…
Power is here,
in cascading tears:
power and knowing
—of the womb,
of the tomb,
of the mystery of tapestry weaving and stitching,
avoiding the precipice of prejudice
and tunneling, digging,
for treasure and safe passage
to the other side.
How deep and wide the journey winds
—through hearts and souls and minds.
How heavy the glory
of the lightest, brightest tears
that fall to wash my spectrum soul
and reclaim it, hale and whole.

I Was Not Alone
by Heather Awad

It was spring
the sun brightened
the flowers on my bedspread
kept watered by the heavy flow
of tears that gushed from my eyes.
Tears that would never end
from a heartache so tangible
it built a home inside me.
I prayed it would release

its clutching hold, freeing
a pain that burrowed
deep in my soul, consuming
my weak-beating heart
polluting my fragile veins.
My woeful cries were not
heard until a brilliant light
answered in those darkest
desperate hours,
come to assuage my pain
apply healing warmth
to this lump of despair
growing inside my chest
becoming a cancer
on my inner peace;
a wound so deep
the scar may never heal.
But the light, it came
It comforted
and I knew I wasn't alone.

Being Seen
by Carolyn Riker

How easily
she could disappear
and still say, she was fine.

Against her will,
her heart,
could transform
into any shape.

Suppressed and repressed
an interlocking fugue
concealed and tucked away.

Spilling from her left
scooping with her right
in an endless attempt
to hold her ghosts

Learning the art of comfort,
quietly, she rested
a wounded heart often
implodes and explodes.

A breeze, rocked her weary.
the rain, pelted her
stinging raw skin.

No longer abandoned in her stories,
the pages flipped through,
a freeze-framed kaleidoscope,
didn't erase but gave some meaning.

The only color to remain was scarlet,
still pumping a fervent drumbeat
in her veins.

Maya
by Taya Malakain

I have worn out my heart
with all of this longing.
My feet ache from the
endless searching.
My legs have dropped me
down to the earth
in complete surrender.

In this quiet stillness,
I realize my folly.

Everything I have been searching for
was within me.

I had been seeking the seeker.
My mind turns in on itself
and there is nothing left for me to do
but laugh.
Laugh so hard the tears roll down
and soften the sweet earth beneath me.

At Dusk
by Alise Versella

At the violet hour
The bougainvillea wilts
The oleander poisons
The men walk by on stilts
The flowers sweat
Deep between their pollen breasts
Like the women who sweat
Between their legs at night
Entangled in ghost limbs of lovers
Who are never coming back to life
Enchanted stems entwined;
They are vines
Ebbed with thorns these roses are
Martyrdom came quickly
To she who was in love
Disparaging the frost in early spring
The sun in golden armor
Stabs with emerald blades
Sprouts feathers plush upon your mound
Where lying lips silence any sounds
Course wings encase a dying heart
And bite marks trail your neck and arms
They etch across your ivory flesh
Like the ink that wraps 'round his forearms
Marble, raven-black like your eyes
With white veins; bloodshot now

Held open wide
Will never again know the pain of a smile.

The Pain of Love
by Catherine Ghosh

It enters me like a phantom
The injection of pure pain
On mournful mornings
When I hear my heart in the lonesome hoots of a barn owl
Winding in sluggish turns through winter fog
Long before the sun rises.

Not mere discomfort,
Like the prolonged silence in elevators,
The flattening, heat-infected summers
Blushes that follow compliments
That tight pair of shoes bound for goodwill,
But instead, it's that raw, squeeze-you-'till-you-break pain:
You know it as well as I do.

And it's not the pretty pain either
That dissipates with swift rewards
After your ears are pierced, or your blood is drawn,
Or fire stings through your wet oven-mitt,
Pumpkin spice swirling into cozy corners.

No, it's not that pretty pain at all,
The kind that fizzles out when you inhale, slowly,
That latches on your nipples in a mischievous toddler's bite
Or rips through your flesh in birthing ten-pound babies.
Swelling your bosom with an "I can do this" breath,
No, it's pain that does you instead!

It's the kind of pain that makes me wonder
If I exist at all under its weight
Inside the rubble of its earthquakes

Tucked into the deep fault lines that
Whither my foundations
Blowing in the dust of prickly perspectives
I once held dear:
Suddenly, I'm only powder whipped by wind.

And I want to trace it out: this pain
Perhaps to a dusty, half-baked trauma
Or baggage I was meant to leave on the carousel
Stuffed with old regrets or infected wounds
Oozing with bits of me I have yet to forgive,
Dreams I have yet to let go of.

Yet this pain flows through me in elusive ways
Wiggling out of my tight definitions
With a suspicious, mischievous velocity
That leaves my sails of self tattered, tattered,
So that I'm only a rag ravaged by the wind
Against its oceanic might.

Do you know this pain?
That truth-chisel that sculpts your heart
Chip, chip, chipping away at all the parts of you
That are made of fear instead of love?

That's when I begin to suspect,
As this stubborn pain in my chest swells
like volcanic soup burning in my soul
That it must be a tool in divine hands,
Masquerading as the undesirable
In response to every time my heart ever longed,
Ached, begged
To know pure love, enduring love,
Rich, delicious sacred-kind-of-love
The kind that apparently needs to break me first,
And shake me first,
From all my winter slumbers
That swirl me mercilessly

into the lonely hoots of the barn owl
Long before the sun rises.

Not Saved
by Jenn Grosso

Those days
When we carry a heavy heart
And sadness wells up inside
The tears pour out uncontrollably
We hope for salvation.
This notion of being saved
It doesn't come from the outside
And it's not about saving ourselves
From discomfort
But with every painful emotion
We can release our grip
Onto expecting it to go away.
Instead
See that we are meeting our teacher
And honor the humanness
That brings us to our knees.
Know that place inside
Unaffected by the mind's waves
That sees us as beautifully
Part of it all
Not needing any saving.

Wreckage
by Tammy T. Stone

On a misty evening past rain,
with dusk giving way to the
blanket of a cloudless night, I
lower my head, as though
for a moment I can turn

away, and wait for the
voices to come wafting
up from the ground, through
open windows onto hollowed
land. The night is long. I would not hide:
I cannot resist their cries the
way bamboo hushes to withstand
the rough winds of a stormy
afternoon. I tremble under the weight
of their pleas; my heart has songs
in it they have heard countless
times before, a refuge for
dreams torn and plundered.
We merge within the vast,
cracked landscape of my
chest, hoping, together, to appease
long, stranded generations, if
for a moment. It comes to this:
the piercing shrieks of
the wounded clawing deep
within until I fall to my knees,
begging forgiveness, for midnight's
love lost, searching wildly for
nature's arms, for love enduring,
to let them fly, and free them
from the wreckage and release
me like a soft forest creature
fumbling in fright through the
war of first night into the
fragile new light of day.

This Does Not Belong To You
by Salyna Gracie

Ask yourself
As you stand there
In the pale grey air

Frozen to these four walls
Feet turned to stone
Decide!
What is worth saving?

Can you will your hands
To grab the memories
You carry only in your heart
Can you pack your boxes full
With the laughter that rings in your ears

The clouds taunt you
Hurry!
There is no time left
Three red flags declare your fate
The defiance of your feet
The moan caught in your throat
Your hands still empty

A Great Unknowing
by Sally MacKinnon

There is a cottage garden planted on Wangerriburra Country;
meditating at dawn, I hear the bees flirting with flowers and
the birds, the birds!
Singing love stories of the universe,
giving voice to the trees touching blue
as the sun spins the Giant Water Wheel.
My hip flexors groan and lift – the spine, the neck
my skull blossoms but
the Gomeroi Mob can't sing up their Country any more
where whitehaven coal rips the guts out of Gaia at Maules Creek.

It is the time of Great Unknowing.
How do we hold huge paradox with our bare hands?
I wake to a world of more beauty, more joy, more love, more peace
than I ever bargained for

and Tibet falls.
I surf with dolphins in the big blue
and the seasons shudder.
I don't know… anything… anymore…
except there is love…
and hate…
and courage…
and fear…

In the park where we gather to honor the weather
there is a ragged paperbark tree whose
shreds waver in the wind
like prayer flags
sounding the sacred
in the suburbs.

The Vase
by Krista Katrovas

I hold the vase you made,
cream colored with daisies
and butterflies, indentions
you carved into wet clay.
I cup it gingerly,
possibly the last thing you created,
before giving it away.
Killed in 1987,
my best friend, cousin,
only one year younger than me,
I walk through life
missing you,
searching for my
best female friend,
yet always feeling left alone.
We wore one another's shoes,
switching one for the other,
wearing mismatch,

feeling completed by the exchange,
knowing no matter where we were
we were walking in one another's shoes.
Like those half golden heart charms
girls wore back then
around their necks,
with, "Best," written on one half,
"Friend," on the other,
completed only when together.
We exchanged
a half a pair of shoes,
because we were too poor for hearts.
Your initials, "K.G.,"
carved by maybe a pen,
or the tip of an unwound paperclip
etched on the bottom of your vase,
is the only tangible thing I have of you,
as I sit panging
within my memories of you, us.
I search through life,
for a life girlfriend
to fill this void,
while holding your empty vase,
knowing that butterflies
are soul birds
and that maybe your young heart
knew this before me somehow,
and why you left them
and my favorite flower,
daisies, behind for me.

Marooned
by Ginny Brannan

When all falls dark upon this world
the daylight lost to hardened night
our compass stuck within a void

our sails slip tattered and unfurled.
When even moon can't guide our course
the clouds have swallowed all its light;
and waves are stilled to silent calm
our hope abandoned on the shoals.
When ink has robbed us of our sight
despondency infests our bones
we stave the dark to wait for dawn…
for in that light the shadows flee—
we mend the sails, reset our tack…
the soft warm breeze soothes like a balm;
we stem the tide to carry on.

2

Voicing Healing

"The place of true healing is a fierce place. It's a giant place. It's a place of monstrous beauty and endless dark and glimmering light."

Cheryl Strayed

Healing as Transformation
by Alice Maldonado Gallardo

How do you heal a sick body, a broken heart, a lost soul? Have we forgotten that the body, heart, and soul are interconnected, and that we are also part of Nature? Six years ago, a doctor informed me that I had five years left to live after being diagnosed with a rare, autoimmune disease called Systemic Scleroderma. There is no medical cure for this illness. Some may say that six years ago, I entered Hell. However, it was an awakening, a transformation that led me on a healing journey to find myself. And it was in this universe inside that I have been able to learn and begin to understand the universe outside.

It has been through agonizing pain and loss that I learned to find the strength to survive. I have also been a dialysis patient since 2011, on a waiting list for a kidney transplant. The road I have traveled since that fateful day of the diagnosis six years ago, has taken me close to death more than a few times. I have also met a lot of other patients in the hospitals, nursing homes, rehab centers, and dialysis centers that have not survived. Why do some people heal while others deteriorate and die? Why do people call me a miracle case, for example?

I believe in miracles. But miracles only occur if you believe with every cell of your being. It is not enough to say a prayer: you have to *feel it* in every cell of your body. You have to transform yourself, your body, your heart, your soul, into an open recipient to feel the Universe, God, Goddess, (any name is fine). Do not think too much about it, you only have to free yourself to feel it.

Transformation, or change, is necessary for healing. There is a reason why change is the only constant in the universe. It is the evolution of God. It is always searching for a balance, an equilibrium of forces. When we lose our balance in life, we get sick. When we lose our balance in a relationship, we end with a broken heart. And when we lose our balance with the world, we lose our way in life.

Physical, emotional, and spiritual pain shatter our soul into pieces that get lost in the dark. It takes a lot of strength to transform hell into heaven. The magnificent power of Nature is there to help you accomplish that. You are never alone, you just have to believe: Believe in whatever belief you have, as long as you believe it with all your being. That will give you the power to heal, to transform, and to wake up into a more balanced, healthy life.

It's been my experience that any creative endeavor will help you find that balance: music, writing, painting, any of the arts! They are all connections to the divine. And when you can make that connection to the divine, then you can heal. That is how miracles occur. That is why some people heal even when the odds are against them, and it is also why some others do not.

I've been attracted to poetry since I was a young child. Poetry has connected me to myself, and the divine in an intimate, powerful way as I express my pain, loss, love, hopes, fears, and in doing so, find the courage to explore life and find balance. Poetry has therefore become a powerful part of my healing.

Healing is a process of transformation in which you believe first and foremost that you *can* heal, because you are never alone: the divine light is within you. Find it, explore it, and feel it through the poetry written in these pages. Feel the healing of your body, your heart, and your soul. Feel how this poetry transforms you as you travel through each of the personal truths of every poet included here. Let them be your guides to the universal truths that reveal themselves to you as you read: that love is divine, and that love heals.

Shamaness
by Nirvani Teasley

Woman, you are me, and I you
Stand up! Awaken to your wild imperium
Grand lady, sister mine
Let wisdom be your docent
Whispering on the wind, listen
Walk among the trees, call him friend
Sit under the Birch, the wild Oak,
He has something to impart to you, Woman
'Go Shamaness, and heal the earth'

Woman, I am calling to you
Come Warrioress, baptize yourself
In Nature's *shakti*, and know the world
Lies within your belly, the cosmos
Dormant in your spine,
And your spirit cannot be broken,
Rise to your power Woman
You are Goddess Divine…

Engulfed
by Shailie Dubois

Sometimes I fall
like a glass held high above my head
It drops
shattering my falseness
pouring out truthfulness
In that moment
I lay silently on the floor
a little lighter
a little calmer
I marvel at the loss
that has engulfed me in magic.

Rise Up!
by Jesse James

There is room for healing
not solely from within passiveness
or gentility;
rather as a constant action
an art

it is revolutionary:
both personal, individual
and, worldwide

necessary
within every movement
on the front lines
putting in the work
and rising
rising alongside those in the fight

we cannot retreat within systems;
those that entrap us
then pretend we are resolving things
not long-term
doing so
we are only treating symptoms
allowing the underlying cause to roam

medicine doesn't work that way
it's not how healing becomes
it means little
if we do not combine those efforts
to something further than ourselves

injustice is an illness
it is a plague
devastating the world

one we must rise above!

we have these gifts for a reason:
we are meant to help heal the world

within us is the resolve
the resolution

together we stand as one.
"rise up" I say to you, healer

rise up and take charge of your gifts.

Blue Green Compass
by Laura Kutney

I sail towards enduring gestures of the sea
Unwavering ebb and flow
Celebrating each brilliant silver moon phase of
Eternal and irrefutable episode of tide
Keeping time of moments and eras alike

Within the sea, detectable and unrevealed elements
Of imminent shoreline and enduring deep waters

Infinite polished granules make the sandy terra firma
Shaped by eons of abounding wave surges
Made over, and over, and over, and over, and yet once more over again
Each wave unique
Never repeated

Beautiful colors and light dancing on the water's surface
  Appearing serene upon the horizon, yet a raucous line where sea and shore meet
  Beneath the calm distance and dynamic swells
  Dwell secrets kept from those above

Now moving past the edge of the water and wading in waist deep
Beyond threshold of sand, luminous azure blue swells and frothy
  foam
Into the gritty, underwater terrain of nomadic sand crabs
I burrow my feet and curl my toes into their shifting homes
Strengthening and bracing myself in my mysterious aquatic bath

Unbending, I wait
One, two waves

I hold steadfast
A third wave reaches out and then withdraws
White spray, grainy sand and salty water mixing into my nose,
  eyes and mouth
The salty tears of the sea are realized

I recognize myself as a grain of sand
Dependant upon receiving equal tumble and polish of my body,
  mind and spirit

Each of life's moments
Weathers my soul
Into the person I am becoming.

Grace
by Camellia Stadts

Not just when the moon wanes,
Should we shed what doesn't belong.
But every evening as the sun goes down
We need to do the same.
To continue grasping for that which has dried to dust
Only makes our souls wither.
Eyes that only look down and see
What has long been gone will never see
The sun or the new growth that springs
from the earth. Never allows the healing touch

That only the sun can provide to the earth, to our souls
Look up, lift your hands and be healed.
We may never learn why things come into
Our lives and why they can't stay, but to
Try to hang on is destructive in every way.
When our hands are raised they can be filled with
New things, beautiful things, joyful things.
How long will they stay, who can say?
Every moment is grace. Don't waste it.
Once you understand that everything changes
Including yourself, you can learn to stay
Right here in this present moment and smile.
Did you know that it's your smile that causes
The sun to shine?

Whole
by Alise Versella

It only hurts if I let it
If I suffer silently soon this too will pass
And from my pain the aftermath is always beauty
From my pain come a million and one lightning bugs
Sparkling like stars spread out against the night
I only feel the hunger until I let it subside
My desire stemming from loneliness
My passion whips around like a fire
Out of control
Come appease it just to tease it
Form the clay to fit inside your mold
Until the edges bleed out
Fix the cracks
And peeling plaster
Cover the holes with spackle
It will only kill me if I let it
But it doesn't
So I am stronger
These ghosts can't haunt me if I don't believe

Don't believe in your nightmares
I run but not from monsters
Not from the past
I run not to keep the pace with others
I run but not away
I run only to see how far
I can get before there's nowhere left to go
I breathe to fill my lungs
Not to bring you back to life
So my ribcage walls cannot come down
Unless I let them fall
This body will only break if I let you snap the bones
And since you have taken no more
Than my heart
It's apparent that I can never fall apart.

When You Think
by Ulli Stanway

When you think you won't make it
You can't get through all of this pain
When you have reached your inner darkness
When you think you want to sleep forever
When you are sure that you are so alone, so very alone
When you look up and the sky is clouded
When you feel this deep hurt, more than words could ever say
When you are in the winter of life
You look up and you slowly open your tired eyes
You see the first ray of sun
You notice that the plants that have recently died are now growing
   again
You notice a little blossom—maybe purple
You start to see beauty
You will see a bird flying in the sky, effortless and joyous
You open up
You decide that you see beauty
In everything and everyone

You meet today
You notice that roses grow
all around you
The sun comes out
A flock of white birds flies over you
The sky open up
You notice the ever-changing seasons
You notice the flow of the water whilst the sunlight covers it in diamonds
You pick up a shell from an empty sandy beach
You hear and you feel
You smell and you sense
It is all here for you—for you and your healing
One thought at the time
One beautiful moment at the time
There is no rush: you have so much time
And slowly, ever so slowly you begin to awaken
Leaving your pain and grief behind
Be gentle with yourself and your tender heart
When you think you won't make it
Life calls you back with gentle subtleness
When you think you won't make it
Open your eyes; the world is waiting for you
Your love is needed
It is time to heal
And time to let go
Life is yours
Bathe in its splendor and beauty
Life is here—for you
Always.

Unchained, Unbound, and Free
by Jackie VanCampen

I felt the shame
Coursing through my veins
Poisoning my being

Contracting my heart
A shame which I did not understand
A shame that persecuted my freedom
Leaving me in pieces
The shame ran so deep
And fragmented my soul
Crumbling my possibilities
And burying my essence

I wondered how
This shame so deep
Could ravage my body
Corrupt my mind
Eat away at my heart
Like a locust
This shame that plagued
My DNA

I had to find a way
To eradicate its root
From the soil of my soul
And free not only me
But the lineage
From which I was birthed

And so it began
The cracking open of my heart
Diving deep into its cave
Exploring each crevice
Bringing light into the darkness
Letting in the healing power of forgiveness
Serving as ointment for my soul
Healing each wound
Smoothing each scar
And as I looked up
I saw the clear, blue sky
Feeling the warmth of the sun
Reminding me of life

The life that I can now create and live
Unchained, unbound, FREE.

Mon Amie
by Mariann Martland

Fly with me in pouring skies,
in spinning fields, like
angels.
Soar below the roaring stars,
through waterfalls and
breathing.
Stumble over flickering black,
with splintered sparkles, my
daytime.
Tempt me into paradise,
down darkened alleys, but
dancing.
Flee with me to private night,
in painful splendor, now
feeling.
Lower us into blissful slumber,
under twinkling dust, find
healing.

Red Ribbon
by Shailie Dubois

Stones beneath the water
Ring like cool bells in a church tower
Rippling the surface to encircle her toes
Ankles
Thighs
Waste
Chest

From the belly
A red ribbon flows
Down the stream
Luring a nearby dove
By it's soulful sway

Plucked from the water
and pulled into the sky
The ribbon is lost to the Son

With the piercing cry
Of a thousand Angels
The Son breathes life
Into her heart
Unfolding
A crown of rose and thorn

Red petals trickle downstream
Where once the red ribbon flowed.

Letting Myself Go
by Ruth Calder Murphy

Yes—
I'm letting myself go!
The once-caged,
would-be wild thing that I am,
the bold, bright and beautiful thing,
with wrinkles and crinkles and folds that sing
of Life.
Yes: I'm letting myself go—
to the four winds, to fly,
to pot, to sleep and dream
and to seed, to blossom all over again.
Yes; I'm letting myself go,
and no! I do not owe myself to anyone,
to keep myself in,

scrubbed and trimmed,
painted and slim,
well-kempt and presentable
like some prized vegetable,
whilst my beauty outgrows
the eyes of those particular beholders;
Yes: I'm letting myself go—
and I want all the world to know
that I don't care one whit what they think of it—
what they think or say when they look and see...
I'm letting myself go—
I'm letting myself grow older and bolder and more wondrously
Me.
Yes, I'm letting myself go;
I'm letting myself BE
—and the whole world can like it or lump it,
scorn it, applaud it, discuss it and score it,
like some kind of social judiciary...
I'm letting myself go.
Yes - I'm letting myself go.
I'm letting myself,
finally,
go free.

The Hungry Ghost
by BethAnne Kapansky

I will tell you the secret
to wellness, and it will
be the simplest yet
hardest thing you
will ever do.

Be yourself.
Pure you.
That is all.

Walk into the world as the real
you, not the version who comes
programmed and packaged
to protect from other people,
prove to other people,
please other people.

Be the you inside who keeps
knocking hard and urgently
trying to find an exit strategy
to escape the well defended
walls holding you back.

You will have to slough off
the residue from others skins,
a careful exfoliation of tender soul,
until you are left with no artifice
and become an author of your
own truth, crafting a rich
narrative to define your
genuine space.

This may come with a cost
for it will require the sacrifice
of warm illusions for colder truths,
and truth can be a lonely road.
But with each brave step you
will step towards your truest of
Norths and find the exquisite life
you create on the outside start
lining up with the exquisite
self you honor on the inside.

You may feel at times like
the hungry ghost, nose pressed
against the bare glass of a room
filled with a banquet of easy.
And though you know such feast

will not offer true sustenance for
your hungry heart, you can't help
but yearn for the delicious luxury
of the road already taken.

Just know that any true dark
night of the soul is here to help
burn through all that isn't real, so
you have only the purest of materials
left to help forge your heart into
a formidable temple of love.

A time may come when you
have to break your heart in order
to save your heart. For the contents
it's formed itself around are not the
contents of the authentic you,
and they suffocate your spirit's
airway so she cannot inhale the
grace tinged sky she requires
for breath.

You will tug and pull and try
to extract her from the sticky
tentacles that keep trying to
reattach and take your heart back to
lesser. Until one day you finally have it
free enough to hold up high then bravely
smash, so you can sort through the
wreckage and finally reclaim your
fragile seeds of self.

A time may come when life
breaks your heart for you and
like a lightening bolt of change,
you find the ground upon which
you once stood ripped from the
certitude of your scrambling feet,

as tiny pieces of self scatter among
a sea of change and you are forced
to leave the safety of shore to go
deep sea diving and retrieve
your precious pearls.

And you will learn somewhere
amidst the deep currents, that the
ocean is so wholly alive with beautiful
terror and awesome wonder, you will
forever be diving to find more pearls
to adorn the treasure chest that now
houses a heart, shining so bright with
radiant luster, people ask what is your
secret and you say with absolute authority,
It is well with my soul.

I will tell you the secret
to wellness, and it will
be the simplest yet
hardest thing you
will ever do.

Be yourself.
Pure you.

That is all.

For all the times... I thank you!
by Sandra Allagapen

For all the times
You let me down,
I thank you
It helped me discover my inner strength

For all the times
You criticized me behind my back

I thank you
It taught me to ignore gossip

For all the times
You turned away from me
I thank you
It encouraged me to allow new people into my life

For all the times
You copied what I had and did
I thank you
It highlighted everything about me that others appreciated

For all the times
You couldn't look me in the eye
I thank you
It showed that I wasn't the one out of integrity

For all the times
You tried to make me wrong
I thank you
It motivated me to be the best I can be

For all the times
You've done your best to keep me small
I thank you
It taught me to value myself

For all the times
You chose not to love me
I thank you
It pushed me to learn to love myself

For all the times
You tried to clip my wings
I thank you
It made me even more determined to fly.

3

Voicing Shadows

"Shadows go in front of you, leading into your future,
and trail behind you, leaving a part of you in the past.
They are clearest when we are in the light,
and disappear when we lose ourselves in darkness."
Kiersten White

Dancing With our Dark Sides

by Anita Grace Brown

A shadow does not have a polar opposite; it gently embraces both light and dark at once. While light displays morning, and darkness mourning, shadows show us that both of these extremes exist simultaneously and in relation to each other. This is true of all polarities, and yet the shadow has none. The shadow, therefore, hints at the inherent unity in everything, and the poetry in this chapter reflects this with graceful, fearless strokes.

Maybe it's the Scorpio in me but I've never found shadows to be scary or menacing. As an only child, I was even known to play with my shadow on occasion. For shadows can be lively and engaging: interplay of the ethereal qualities of light with the denseness of matter, which thereby produces an image. Often created by nature's dance—a tree limb bouncing, leaves swaying, a bird flying past the sun, our own bodies moving—shadows are naturally captivating!

As children, we do not question the intimate relationship we have with our shadows. When we move our limbs, our shadow's limbs move: our awareness of this is pronounced. As we grow older, however, we humans have a tendency to shy away from our "shadow selves". In Jungian psychology one's shadow self is a metaphorical reference to the unconscious mind: the place in which we store all the "dark half of the human totality". It represents our un-lived life: the good and the bad in the necessary cycle of loss and renewal.

Shadow denial is a form of psychological repression, and as anyone with even a passing familiarity with psychoanalysis can tell you, what is repressed seeks revenge. We can see this being mirrored in the physical realm every day as each of us must continually surrender to the inevitable pains of being human. Consequently, many of us have come to unconsciously deny our physicality in an effort to avoid pain.

Over time, this avoidance has translated into contempt and diminution of the body in our western culture. We have lost the loving connection to the body and become two-dimensional. We swing between extremes like a pendulum, and have lost our intimacy with the unifying shadows. Within this disconnection our bodies have unfortunately become places we use to deposit our fear, shame, grief, etc., surfacing in struggles like eating disorders, addictions, and other forms of self-harm.

In Thich Nhat Hanh's famous piece "Please call me by my true names", the poet embodies three selves: an innocent, a sinner and a witness. They each ask us to look within our nature and shed light on the baser parts of the unconscious self—our own capacity for violence, jealousy, and greed, trusting that the fiery light of consciousness desires to transform and enlighten.

Similarly, we find this same concept in the Hindu goddess Kali, who celebrates the shadow side of humanity by giving it full expression, in the belief that within such primal release rests the doorway to deeper self-awareness.

Like goddesses wielding their own weapons to unlock the darkest secrets of their own consciousness, the poets in this chapter unite to give voice to the shadows. Thus the shadow is exposed to the light of consciousness and ceases to be the destructive force it was when dismissed. Instead of residing in the depths of the unconscious, the shadow gains its rightful place as a function of the creative personality, for some of the greatest artistic masterpieces have been birthed from shadows. In doing so, pain is reconciled and redeemed. Such alchemical processes restore our golden inner life, and the phoenix rises from her ashes, as we watch these women playing with their shadows, like fearless children. I invite you to take part in the game, and bring your shadow with you!

"Light and dark:
To know both, to embrace both
Is to live
Is to know

Ourselves,
Others,
God."

W. Carpenter

Listen
by Ruth Calder Murphy

Listen.
There's a voice in the darkness
—and it's mine.
A tiny voice,
murmuring wisdom and truth,
beautiful and bright
like just-before-dawn light
on the new-born babbling of a mountain stream,
freshly freed from the rocky dark—
and all the epiphanies of the Dreaming
in its song.
Listen—
it's the song of sea and sky,
the song of knowing without knowing why
—the song with Stardust in its spirit
and Earth in its soul—
and in the gloom,
it's susurrating, murmuring,
filling the void
and making me,
somehow,
whole…
There's a voice in the darkness
and it's mine.
A voice outside of space and time,
somehow,
outside of here and now—
but absolutely now and absolutely here,
and I will listen,
and in the gradual dawning,
I will hear—
my own voice,
rising with the early morning lark,
embracing possibility
and banishing the dark.

In The Winter of My Undoing
by Sonja Marie Phillips- Hollie

It was the winter
of my undoing,
It was the silencing
of my soul.

As I laid down with destiny
covered in a white veil
of delusional snow
angels wept,
the nuns slept.

As intrusive thoughts of him
crept into my window:
Sonnets of despair
underneath my pillow.

Loneliness at my door—
I let her in,
she wrestled with my soul
unleashing the pain
of a faded memory.

Outside the pristine walls
of this convent
I am haunted by a love
that was never meant to be.

As I walk my own path
I run through the barren trees—
crushing vintage leaves,
surrendering to the frigid winds
of change inside of me.

Alas, my heart is set free
as I bid farewell

to the apparition
I once loved.

As the winter of my undoing
came and went,
So did,
the pain and sorrows
of my inner torment.

From Inside the Tower
by Kai Coggin

My winged heart is in a tower,
I peer through barred tiny window
to see the patch of blue sun,
a breath of sky dancing shadows on the wall,
I become the window,
the overarching stone that lies on the cusp
of inside and out,
of cold and everything that is giving birth as spring,
I become the wall,
kiss my own shadows until they no longer
join my feet and merge into me,
they are free winged things,
circling overhead as a chorus of angels
not serpents,
no, not dark,
not gargoyles that laugh at this delusion,
this tower is a closed mouth,
is a closed cell, and all of my cells are locked inside,
no place to divide, no music of spiritual mitosis spreading
its melodies on the waves of zephyrs,
only stasis, emotional inertia,

the infinite depths of Love
are all that can hear to the deep belly of my cries,
and through the keyhole of the padlock

that holds me in this pensive and sullen eternity,
I can hear the faint roaring of a dragon's breath,
with enough fire to melt
whatever mechanism is keeping me here.

When all illusion
is melted into a liquid gold pool,
and I emerge unscathed,
I see that the tower
was always
my sky-reaching ribcage,
my winged heart
holding every birdsong,
my arms, my hands, unchained and open.

Impossibility
by Ruth Calder Murphy

Impossibility
is the darkening of hope—
the tightening of the noose
as the rope drops,
the smashing of the infrangible atom;
the devil set loose.

Impossibility
is the inability to see
the possibility
of escape—
or to divine the shape
of freedom.

Impossibility divides,
turning off all the lights,
and hides in the shadows
of self-fulfilling-prophesy'd nights.

Impossibility is the death of hope
—and love and faith;
the wraith of life.

And so I choose to dwell
—to Be—
alive in Possibility;
it's why the caged bird sings in me:
She'll dream, and dream eternally,
of Freedom.

The Solitary Journey
by Charu Agarwal

I came alone
and shall go alone—
this to me is known.
then why en-route
do I now and then moan,
longing to find a clone?

My soul so pristine
is content and serene,
knowing deep within—
I am my sole kin.
Yet my heart seems to seek
others to bond with and speak.

But, is it a surprise?
As I awaken and arise,
setting sail on my boat,
eyes on the distant shore—that
those still in the dream
now should strangers seem?

When I Feel Like I Am Falling From My Soul
by Maureen Meshenberg

when I feel,
like I am falling
from my soul,
hanging on by a strand—
I free fall,
and let go deep—
into my wondering,
it takes my breath,
as I grasp—
to reach to that place,
of being redeemed—
but it is not about,
redemption—
or the right and wrong,
of it—
the pit in my stomach,
from the ache of it—
catches me off guard,
all that's left is to
hold to my dark,
but love's light comes,
and brings me back—
not because I am perfect,
or because I followed
the right steps,
I just reach up—
and open up enough,
to let what is true
flow through me,
love saves me—
when I feel abandoned,
confused,
defused,
alone…

brings me and cradles me,
in arms of wholeness—
back to my soul,
back home.

Sleepless Night
by Mel Martin

Silver moonlight all around,
mist floating off the ground,
eerie owlets hoots and squeal,
as shadows turn to nightfall.

Chilling fear within my heart,
tells me: "From this path depart!"
keeping silence deep within,
and the darkness of each sin.

Deafening screeching far off yonder,
distracts my soul enough to ponder,
if I ever again see the light,
and get through this blackest night.

Golden sunbursts light the heaven,
announcing dawn will soon awaken
from her slumber, bringing peace
dancing beams proclaim: "Night, cease!"

Rhododendron Mile
by Lisa Smith

(An ode to separation and displacement)

A drop in the pool of life's lost years
A reflection in the mirror of a child's smile
But that's what was and you are here

And it only seems such a little while…

Like Moths attracted to fire's glow
Dicing with danger in a mystic way
Dancing sparks fire up the night
But all is lost in the break of day…

The sun shines brightly on a fresh morn
The birds they harmoniously sing
Flowers pushing, through the earth budding
But it's the end of Autumn not Spring

Angels Above
by Taruni Tan

Do you see
the darkness in my soul?
Then you'll understand
why I do not dream,
why I'm not free
and only partially whole.

I'm mad in a way,
I think of death
more than life,
I was a wife
and now I grieve
for the one who left.

From across the great ocean
you saw my face,
Who can say
why you were chosen
to take his place
and bid me welcome.

If I appear ungrateful
and sadness remains,

Forgive me, I'll laugh in time
and heal the pain if you
remind me please
that it's not in vain.

Carry me this night
away from sorrow,
Spin me a tale
that I can follow
Thru' cold wind and fog
into a new tomorrow.

Embrace me close
and sing to me,
That we'll grow old
so I can believe, and
Make me a promise
that you'll never leave.

I'll be yours forever
I'll take your pain,
your name,
your best and worst,
And love you freely
forgetting life's curse.

Angels up there if you are watching,
Listen close and spread your wings,
For I will sing to you of wondrous love
and forget for a moment the one above,
Angels spread your wings,
fly us home when our time comes.

Ghost Train
by Julia W. Prentice

I hear the ghost train whistle
Echoing through the past

Its lonesome wail encompasses
The heartfelt doom inside
Leftovers from the shredded history
Known as my story, my undoing
See the indelible marks ride on
Stains of guilt and shame
For things both done and undone
Stains no bleach of regret removes
Marks unforgiving and of unforgiveness
So the train thunders on
Tracks are rusty from the tears
Fallen in the ashy dust of long ago…
Does the engine ever cease?
Cargo of loneliness and fear
Anxiety and deepest sadness
Carried on forever
Car by car they pass
My sight blurred by the wind
And burning remorse
Whence goes this train?
It travels in my soul.

How I Bleed
by Kathi Valeii

I have been afraid of you all of my life.
All of you.
Even You, the one with a goddess heart, big and deep and gushing
    with life.
The one who says,
"all of the women I love know how to bleed with me."

Especially you.
You scare me the most.

You have touched something that I can't find.
A thing unnamable, unreachable, indiscernible to me.

You illuminate my insecurities, you expose the frailty and failures of Women.

Women who are dominated by masculine motivators with fake, feminine veneer.
Women who distinguish themselves by which ones of us they are not.
Women who don't know who they collectively are.

How can we possibly bleed together?

You, who cut me while I gave birth.
You, who grabbed my baby and yelled how selfish and stupid I was.
I can still feel that puncture wound deep in my chest.

I bled alone that day;
from every orifice, I bled.

You, who said I used the "wrong" voice; the not-Your-voice.
How my thousands of hours of work were churned through the meat grinder of your mouth,
drizzled with syrupy sweetness.
As though candy-coating them would entice me; make me want to lick them, believe them.
How the mess of it clung to my hands, sticky and gross, as I turned the doorknob to leave.

This is how I bleed.
Alone.

The time you slashed me with your words then went bat-shit crazy when we talked about it.
Right after our kids' play date.
Right after we drank tea; made awkward conversation.
I readied myself for a weekend away, the sharpness of your words slicing my yoni,
ensuring I would bleed again.

I gushed by myself on the porch swing that day.

You, who took my words to publicly mock me.
Your foot-to-the-throat, "Say Uncle, Bitch," until I erased my
   graffiti and walked away.
I erased your face, and others, too
while I bled
and bled
and bled.

Alone.

On the plane ride, my cup fills and overflows.
I sit alone in the bathroom of that bumpy jet, consider my options.
We like to say that men are messy.
But women are messy as shit.
I will sit in a room full of women.
Women who will make me cry.
In empathic solidarity. And in exclusion.
I will hang my head. Bury my face. I will run to my room.
I will hide.

No woman knows how to bleed with me.

I bleed alone.

I bleed for us all.

This Cynical Heart
by Ginny Brannan

Imagine a place with no pain existing,
where ills that are carried through life disappear.
Like Thomas, this heart is quite bent on resisting,
yet lingering questions insist on persisting;
their answers illusive and ever unclear.

And still I am finding my mind keeps returning
whenever the stillness and quiet appears.
I ponder the purpose of life, disillusioned—
the darkness that settles, no certain conclusion;
for ages I've tarried, alone and austere.

I wonder how long I've withdrawn in seclusion,
closed off from emotion, these goals cast unclear?—
Where cynical thoughts thrive without absolution
despondent, in need of insightful intrusion…
does anyone notice behind this veneer?

In my heart I envision a child that's running
and playing with others, no longer constrained—
surrounded by light of the love that he carries,
his purpose fulfilled, this small emissary
reminds us "Be happy, we'll meet once again."

Everything is Dissolving
by Gwen Potts

Everything is dissolving
Such turbulent waters
Washing my soul
Clean and bear
All is dissolving
Over and over
The cycles of life
Stripping away
Can't bear it again!

Lost sea
Of yesterday's sorrows
Strong, overwhelming tidal waves
That bombard my spirit
Throwing this weary body
Against the rocks of time

Undercurrents drag, twist and hurl
Spinning downward in the undercurrent
Lost in the roughest ocean
Of yesterday's sorrow

Worn out patterns
Revisited yet again
Pain and worry of the past reborn
Fear a very real illusion
Testing an honest spirit
Before new boundaries
Can even hope to be born

Confusion strips away ego
Too tired now to fight
Lost dreams a mere delusion
Everything I thought was right
The right direction, path to follow
Now becoming obliterated
By a huge tidal wave
Of keen inner sight

Letting go
Or giving in?
As the onion sheds another layer
Yet looks so similar to before
Deep sadness pervades my being
All that was once so sure
Is lost in the sea
With no direction
Not knowing
Where, when or how
Or what shore
I will wash up upon
No certainty here at all

If asked to let go
Of all I see

Knowing I have no strength
To fuss or fight
Answerless questions
Just float through my mind
Observing the need
Ego desiring one particular thing
Watch it all pass by
On a cloud of energy
Consciousness morphing
Into whatever
God knows what is best for me.

4

Voicing Light

> "My first memory is of light —
> the brightness of light —
> light all around."
> Georgia O'Keeffe

A Dawning Fullness
by Ruth Calder Murphy

In general, I try to avoid sweeping statements—especially about groups of people. However, I think this one is probably justifiable: that poets—and artists of every kind—tend to have a particular sensitivity, metaphorically speaking at least, to Darkness and Light. This generalization seems to be increasingly confirmed, as I get older and make new connections.

Internal darkness, I would suggest, drives people to create something from it: to make sense of it in words, images and music. The dawning of light on that darkness results in an equally intense paroxysm—a celebration of creativity and the beginning of a new phase.

For myself, I've suffered with a sunlight deficiency condition since I was a child—and our dark British winters, though undoubtedly possessed of a certain beauty, are particularly difficult times for me. I've never been especially frightened of darkness, in and of itself; I've always recognised in it a unique allure, a beauty—even a sort of comfort and safety. The womb-soft darkness of caves and duvets and falling into dreams certainly has its own appeal. Nevertheless, the impact on my life and health of extended periods of darkness has made itself keenly felt. Depression, fatigue and physical and mental malaise leave me longing for golden summer dawns, bright days and late, long-shadowed evenings.

Much of my poetry, then—and my visual art and music, too—has been inspired and informed by this dance of Light and Darkness. I'm convinced that the same can be said of most other artists, writers and musicians: that through our creativity, we express the lesson we've learned, and continue to learn. That is, the importance of letting the light in—both literally and metaphorically—and of letting our own light shine brightly and clearly, even when everything seems dark. That balancing of the darkness with light is, in some ways, what life is all about!

It's been a blessing to read the poems in this chapter, and an honour to contribute to them. As Jamie Burgess says,
"It is time.
To lift our faces
to the sun,
to watch the fear
turn to dust,
to step into
the fullness
of who we are.
Divinity
wrapped in skin."

I think that this is what we do—those of us who read or write poetry—through our interaction with word art and imagery. We lift our faces to the sun and step into a newly-dawning fullness. This new dawn is the Fullness of Being, here and now: the fullness of who we are, where we are—and of living that fullness, fully.

Radiate Love
by Jamie Burgess

We are dimming our light
with these masks.
Tucked away,
so neatly.
Protected.

Hiding,
chasing ghosts and shadows
in the darkness.
Losing touch
with our power.
Burning daylight.

It is time.
To lift our faces
to the sun,
to watch the fear
turn to dust,
to step into
the fullness
of who we are.
Divinity
wrapped in skin.

With courage in our pockets
and our hearts on our sleeves—
allowing ourselves,
finally,
to be seen—
we laugh,
we dance,
we dream.

And then comes
the night,

so full of magic.
We feel
stardust
coursing through our
veins
and starlight
seeping from our
pores.

We feel
every
single
cell.

Radiating.

Ascendance of Light
by Maureen Kwiat Meshenberg

ascendance of light,
warms our summer sky-
rising with brightness,
clothing the day-
with delight.
opens our sky
with illumination-
as we gather in celebration,
the flowering of the-
sun's full bloom.
resting so high,
kissing the night
with the fragrance,
of fire-
we gather our desires,
as they burst-
from our souls,
dancing to the

rhythm of the drums,
they move to the beating-
of our hearts,
we hold ourselves open-
to bring this longest day,
our intentions,
summer solstice-
yes day of all days,
as we unite,
celebrating the sun's
brilliant light,
the chance to take,
the pleasures of warmth and laughter-
celebrating the summer,
with exuberance.

Life That Knows
by Helene Rose

Damp dewy earth
beneath my feet.
The clouds roll in
and I sink to greet
the taste of grass
between my toes
heavens scent
of Life that knows.
Let yourself grow
wild and free like
tall wild grasses that
reach your knee.
Let the wind move you
and dance you
and be
in the space of
your divinity.

Dancing the Dream Awake
by MaRa LuaSa

Luminous Lights,
Reflect The Beat,
Of My Evolving Expanding
Heart.

The Dream Sparks,
The Eyes Of My Feet,
To Activate Beneath.

Movement Pulsates,
Through Internal Spaces;
Pictures And Memories
Embody Through Dance.

Every Cell,
Vibrates,
The Story,
Of Whole Visions,
In All Their Glory.

Bright Eyed,
I Stretch Wide,
The Dream ~
Embodied,
In This Now.
Movement
Shows All,
In This Now
Moment.

The Dream Is Alive;
The Story Expressed.
Oh Yes!

Fireflies
by Danielle Kreps

Fireflies dance close to mother earth in the warm night air
And I find myself seeking out small flames within
Points of beauty where spirit touches down on an open thought
And light intertwines with rivulets of impulse
Cascading out along meridians of desire

My hands holding the warmth of your skin
Connecting with the undercurrents of a life

Gravitating towards the sun.

Planting Stars
by Kai Coggin

I buried a handful
of stars deep into the soil,
scattered diamonds
lighting
everything black,
you know how dirt smells like possibility
when it is just that dirt and your naked fingers?
It's primal.
It's energy.
It's holding something that never ends.
I felt that today.

I will wait to tell you where
I buried the stars,
wait to see if a constellation
can really form
from dust and spit and earthworms and myth.

In a few weeks,
I will go out alone,

no, I will bring you with me,
and we will find an empty space in the night sky,
that all of a sudden becomes a distant tiny sprout of light,
and we will hold our breath,
waiting to see our reflection.

Rainbows and Me
by Charu Agarwal

Should it rain
but yet
be bright;
my heart
does leap
in sheer delight.
I scan the sky
—up, down,
left, right,
hoping for
the elusive sight;
And when I see
the shimmering bow
of subtle colors,
all aglow;
the sublime and
ethereal arc
dazzles me,
making her mark—
touching me
right at my core;
my spark
of innocence
—restored.

Seek the Pearl
by Sara Johansson

Seek the pearl
of wisdom inside your heart,
and you shall unfold
the language of Spirit.

It speaks tales
of a thousand lifetimes spent,
through darkness
and light journeyed.

And as your inner teacher
reveals itself,
you begin to discover
worlds within you,

you never knew existed...

It is the light of your spirit,
coming into full bloom,
as a newly awakened flower
in the midst of spring.

Pearls of the Sea
by Carolyn Riker

Lessons given and unravel
on the cusp of understanding.
The light shelters a heart hidden in the dark.

Letting go of expectations.
Revisiting old traditions and creating new.
We crumble to our knees and
wings shield us from the storms.

Revelations spiral counterclockwise.
Here we find strength in unusual ways.
The magic of our wings,
finds we can soar.

My ship is always sailing,
in a bottle along uncharted seas.
The messages we receive are often subtle but
clearly what we need.

And so we begin this year
with blinks of yesterday leading on a path of now.
We hold the swirling energy
and when ready, sip the streams of wisdom.

It's in the knowing we find the answers.
We breathe the messages and
birth pearls of the sea,
all guided by the stars
found in you and me.

Winged Prayer
by Madhava Lata Dasi

A prayer came on wings
for me,
at once I could not see
the desert of my heart,
the saguaro,
that me,
with its thorns,
ceased to be,
spiritual awareness
lit up everything;
cupped hands
filled with mercy
spread the wings

from petals and leaves
took off to the sky
landed on my soul
in a shower of light,
like a fulfilling kite,
that whisper,
reached far and inside
brought in a whiff of inner delight
the dimmed flame was fanned
to dance more bright;
my mind stopped to think,
emotions floundered
in a speechless tide,
'cause the wave was me,
I could perceive,
stirred up and ruffled
by a love wind.

Your Soul Holds the Flame
by Maureen Kwiat Meshenberg

All that has bruised you,
cannot contain you —
your soul holds the flame,
its fire stands brighter —
against the raging winds,
of life.
light that reaches to touch,
your life around you —
passion not held back,
by one moment that passes —
and tries to blow it out,
from inside you.
your brilliance is forever,
past your own
physical living,
it shines in the

universe of dreams,
constellations of beings
that mingles with your truth.
the light that moves,
through the stories
of you,
melts them all away
from who you truly are.
reaching past the dawn,
of your night
no darkness can
restrain you,
for you are more
than a dim dying star,
you are the source
of your eternal glow,
moving through
like a sun of
a new morning.

As the Movement of Moment
by Jennifer Hillman

As the movement and rhythms of moment's dance
The breath and ease of the beauty within
Grace the heart's everlasting splendors;
Feeling and experiencing the fullness of life.

Embrace it all, dear child of love.
Know that it is all real
And still the illusion
Of your imagination gone wild.
Fully presence in the essence of mind.

Wild and wondrous...
Oh dance oh dance child
With the music in heart

The universe's orchestra is here
And fully charmed.

Move in the breath
And the grace that you are.
Be fully present
And know who you are.

Brilliance, magical and everything else…
Dance with the essence out of mind
Embrace yourself and love…
And all be divine.

Keep Faith
by Ruth Calder Murphy

Keep kindness close,
keep love and light,
keep peace, keep life;
keep burning bright -
until they overflow the bounds of you
and spread to others, passing through
and fill the world around you, too…

Keep space around your mind and heart
that they might breathe and stretch and grow
and feel and know as fits their part
—and flex creative muscles, so
for usefulness and Beauty's art.

Receive, on every inhaled breath,
life's fullness: love, and peace and light;
release, on every exhale, Death—
and rise again, more strong, more bright.

Keep kindness close and let it lead;
Keep faith with Love
and hope, in deed.

5
Voicing Vulnerability

"I hear myself speak words, voices that seem unclear.
Here I sit as if transparent allowing the voices to move
through me. No walls do I see; the windows to my soul
are open to receive. The true nature of being is that I am
exposed, ripped wide open, torn down to the bone.
This hurts, I know, tears cleanse my soul
To allow these voices to be heard allows me to feel whole.
I have accepted the invitation: all is a part of who I am."

Kim Buskala

Our Beautiful Transparency

by Milijana Bozovic

Carry on, dear reader! The journey continues: Before you we spread the scenery of the inner worlds of women. These landscapes are so giant and oceanic that only brave and patient travelers can float upon them. If we surrender to them together, we can learn what encourages the widening and blossoming of each of these intimate expanses.

Shhhh... listen! There is a peaceful echoing of words. Can you hear them? This is what they say: "Freedom is found in releasing our feelings, and courage in letting ourselves be vulnerable. As a result we are given the power to perceive the whole world within us." Therefore, reader, let's be bravely soft, fragile and gentle. It is only in such a state of receptivity that we will be able to truly experience all the feelings that are given to us here, in this poetry.

Here, now, at this part of our shared journey, we are the same in our peaceful essence as we always have been, and yet we are screaming, we are regretting, we are afraid, we are raw and we need protection. We are living through an emotional winter, we are imperfect, we are dark, we are light, we are sailing through the storm and we are exposed to life completely. As you read, you will be able to feel our Sun and Moon, and breathe in their common light. You can feel our ebb and flow, and touch the pearls of words that we left behind when the tides went out.

Peer into these pearls and mirror yourself in our colors, tones, cries and melodies, for they are yours too. Let's be so close that we have no division between each other. Let's be so close that we can see and celebrate one another's sweet vulnerability, for such celebrations pay tribute to what we share. What we all have in common.

Vulnerability is to see ourselves as we are: completely transparent, with our flaws as clear as our virtues. We don't want to be artificially shaped just to be acceptable. Instead, we want to recognize each other by our true, authentic feelings.

Vulnerability manifests itself as the courage to be fragile and frail. It is when we are touching the bottom and we suddenly realize that we are reaching the depths. Within such depths we see that we are surviving, that we have trusting hearts, that we are perfect in our imperfections. We flow and we are not afraid, we are complete, we are released and we surrender to life completely. We are life itself!

Our fears are only temporary things and we can drop them at will. We can break them or live with them as part of us, and even get to know them really well. Whatever we choose to do, whenever we do, we do so without labels. In this unique space of being vulnerable, there comes a time when we feel as if we are sailing in the ocean and we are simultaneously the ocean itself!

So be vulnerable, dear reader. Be brave, so that you can be vulnerable. Be willing to be brittle, and know your weakness. Be afraid and know your fear. Be raw and allow yourself to feel all your desires as they are forming. Be whatever you feel like being and feel free being that. Float and fly, stand and burn, breathe! And, if you want, break your fragility into bits so you can fully shine. Are you still with us, brave reader? I feel you are me, dear reader. Let us be vulnerable together then, together as one.

Raw
by Tracie Nichols

my resilience
is so fragile

grief
shreds it

dead leaves
fluttering anxiously
in frigid winds
torn branches
clutch uselessly
holding to
nothing

I've lost
everything
in small
pieces

outward
picture perfect
inward such
echoing
emptiness

I found myself out

always afraid
others would see
past the mask
unveil the fraud

I did it
to
myself

who am I
now?

I can't do this
anymore
cast-iron competent
face tearing flesh

I can't do this anymore

I doubt everything

no kernel of redemptive
light
burning
inside
this time

no positive words
trip away
from my mouth
to reassure
myself
everyone
who relies on
me

I am lost

I doubt everything

(I know I'm in here somewhere)

what a relief
it is
to show my face
to the world
unsure and small

timid
yearning for
mother-touch

despairing
broken
needing

what a relief
it is
to be just
human
woman.

Of Things That Pass
by Tammy T. Stone

I fall before you, big wind.
I am tired, and need a tree to sit under,
I have been waiting such a long time.
If I can't live there, yet,
on the horizon's far side, I would
like at least to turn my eyes
upward to the sky's streaky,
crimson dreams.

I want to feel beauty's skin
on my skin, a life's sum of the simplest
things, the wild belly laughs of
youth, hair all messed up
from wild play on a fearless day.
I didn't know what I had,
I didn't have the capacity for
acknowledgement.

I have searched long and deep,
entwining with life's decorations,

flirting with emptiness,
that beguiling, sinewy story
that never runs out,
the way I will run out.

I want to start with beauty,

Of things that pass,
wheels of merriment
topping the world.
It's time to build the magic
together, even as I crawl low
to the ground, the sun long set,
where I can fall into
Earth's green embrace,
Soaked after rain, a universe of
Scents, textures and hope.

Vessels
by Shailie Dubois

Can you see,
The beauty that spills from brokenness
freeing the bound
Giving voice to the heart

Can you hear,
The call that echoes in chaos
calming the buzz
Giving peace to the soul

Can you feel,
The rapture no longer contained
Moving the concrete
Giving mystery to life

Shatter the manmade vessels that keep magic docile.

Soul Scream
by Catherine Ghosh

Waxing moon, waning sleep
I sift reality
through a hormonal sieve.

Swelling breasts, shrinking calm
My fringed soul
is mocked by the dawn.

Birds sing, the owls go mute
existential angst
fuels my internal disputes.

Rising orb, descending fears
my parachute rips
before courage appears.

Welcoming tangles, yet shunning the thread
Only scratchy conflict
turns with me in bed.

Dispersed pieces, fragmented light
I am slices of being
hiding from sight.

Snippets of person, scattering about
Connecting the dots
I murder my doubt.

Ambiguous identity, solid theme:
Before I start to bleed
I always hear my soul scream.

Moon wanes, sleep grows
Now I slip into the center
Where peace flows.

Winter Sun
by Lynda Vargas

The winter sun illuminates

different corners of our lives.

The sidelong rays cast warmth and light

in unusual places.

We never saw that vase before,

bathed in such a glow.

The leaves dance on the carpet

in playful shadows.

The framed photograph on the piano lights up a precious face,

and leaves us

breathless.

We must hurry to grasp each moment

with gratitude

before the winter sun moves on

to illuminate yet other corners of other people's lives,

leaving us in the shadows

of our solitude.

Tiny Boat
by Kai Coggin

Today,
I am a tiny boat,
on a huge empty ocean,
with nothing but the longing in the wind
looking for someone to push around,
looking for someone to sing to,
and my ears are open,
but I can't recognize the sound.
I hardly try.
Reaching out towards the sky,
the blue fills me
and I become water,
but I still don't know
which way is up
or which way is down.
A side effect of woman is that
I am tied by my heartstrings
to the pull of sea,
and new moons sometimes
open up old wounds
to let the light in.
My heart floats
even if it's heavy.
On some distant horizon,
a woman with a lighthouse
in her chest
is remembering the sound of my name.
I am a tiny boat,
drifting,
high tides shifting on an ocean of grace.
I'll shoot a flare from my bow,
out into the night
and wait for the stars
to notice
that I am gone.

For now,
I am adrift,
ribcage boat frame anchored
to the rising and daunting crescent.

The Ocean Within
by Kim Buskala

I repeat the
Motion of the ocean
Over and over
The waves keep coming
The tides do change
Highs and lows
I try to allow
Myself to enter
The flow
At times my movements
Are so big
as the crest of a wave
I crash
I fall
I smash against
I land
Only to roll
A gentle roll
On a calm day
Windless
Barely moving
As if to stand still
I breathe in that moment
The still in the movement
Only to know
Winds will carry
Me away
Waves will grow
I may need to hide

Behind barricades
That protect the windows
Of my soul
Eyes void of thought
Questions answered
When the time comes
What really matters?
Lost in self.

Of the Ebb and Flow
by Ruth Calder Murphy

Here I stand,
Darkness kissing my skin chilly
—Me—
balanced and stretched like a tree,
Me, beneath the fullness of the Summer's brightest moon.

Here I bow and reach and shrink and grow,
embracing cycles and circles,
the ebb and flow of
my soul, woven
in and through the choreography of seasons,
the turning of the tides,
the sleeping of my Muse
and the returning of my voice
from spiraling stars,
the mists of Time,
the infinite skies
and dim and distant mountainsides…

Here, I stand,
Night like a blanket
—like a shroud,
like the tomb,
beating with the promise
of the full-term womb -

moon-drenched silent
in the pregnant pause
before Dawn.

Here I stand,
moon-washed and waiting
—once again—
to be born.

In the Dark of Light
by Tammy T. Stone

In the light I play,
porous and awash under sun,
where the colors are more
than they are, strewn upon the ground
in their wildest symmetries—
and I am emerging into
all that I am, until the
sun sees through me
and I can't bring my body to
hold its luminescence—
I close my eyes and wait
for nature's rhythms to carve
smooth this rupture.
Colors and shapes dance ecstatic
before my eyes to their own echo, and in
this shadowy place I retreat,
not quite unafraid, having birthed
in its swell of memories,
certain now that the absence of
earthly hues I've tried to
forge into my skin is
today's calling,
so I enter and rest, soothing
my frantic chest, swimming through
and whispering into the silence

while my bones quiver, threatening to fall—
I reach one hand out to catch
what light I can and hold
the other close to me,
to draw out another
piece of the dark.

Perfect Imperfections
by Kim Buskala

I see a heart
Centered and full
Yellow is my sunshine
Blue is my sky
The storm in the center is my eye
I blink in disbelief
My breath I hold
Virtue pain fear stowed
Outside the brightness
Imperfections are many
Imperfections of life
Illuminated by the sun above
Below we wish to hide
Inside a cave
Ashamed, afraid, flawed
To know our world is full
Of imperfections
Which make our world go around
Perfect imperfections
In retrospect
One is the loneliest number
That you'll ever know
To be lost
With thoughts of not being found
To hide so well
That even your screams are unheard
The bleakness we create

The sun has set
Shadows grow under the moonlit sky
We are forgotten
We are lost
Only to be found
If we allow
Let the darkness
Bring comfort
Quiet stillness
The ground is my cover
I feel found
I find comfort within
Silence
No wind
The storm
No more
Perfect imperfections.

A Trusting Heart
by Camellia Stadts

Can you make it tomorrow?
Can you make it today?
Take just one step
One small step into the future
You don't even have to know
Where you are going
You can have your eyes open or closed
The Spirit leads, so eyes aren't necessary
Only a willing heart, a brave heart
A beautiful, strong trusting heart.

Fear Is The Thing, My Dear
by Charlotte Eriksson

But if your heart doesn't have any fear it will cease to grow
in time
for fear is the thing, dear.

Fear is the thing that makes the heart pump, eyes open and
mind swell,
and fear makes the safety worth chasing. Adventure awaits on the
  other side of that fall,
in that fall,

and if you knew the outcome of each and every thing
the point would cease to be.

Fear is the thing my dear. Fear is the thing
that makes the heart grow.

When a Woman Surrenders
by Helene Averous

When a woman surrenders
She lets go
She lets go of her pride
Of being the perfect one:
Fearless and strong
Committed to the wellbeing of others before all

She allows the flow of tears
Releasing that space
Where no one could enter

And through that moment of Grace
Flowers start to blossom

And the blessing "I love You"
Makes her free
And empty.

6
Voicing Courage

"When I dare to be powerful, to use my strength
in the service of my vision,
then it becomes less and less important
whether I am afraid."

Audre Lorde

The Water of our Soul's Garden
by Carolyn Riker

I found Courage today in snippets of memories cushioned with love. I found her rocking in a corner soothing bruised wings. I found her bravely shaking and shouting, No! Courage is tender as much as fierce. I saw her standing nearby wiping tears I found Courage today as more layers were revealed. Courage replied, "I have always been here."

In our deepest darkest days and nights of despair, when words and thoughts and feelings are teeming in grief, the poetry of words gives us relief.

Between the tissues of sadness, hurt and tragedy, Courage is often rebirthed. It's not a onetime process. Courage recycles; it is a reincarnation through the process of living and dying.

We voice our Courage through our song. It starts as a somber chant as we sing the blues and weep through the crevices of time. We pause to find the meaning and in the end we find Courage to redefine what was tragic into a source of vibrant strength and humble resilient power.

Through our words we transform our weaknesses, stanza by stanza, rhyming or not, until we find the prose that fully hints at the lushest painting from our soul. Courage births creativity. Creativity is fed with courage. The symbiosis is interlocked in a beautiful sway of our hips and hearts. We interlace our fingers around Courage and hold it dearly.

We write our poems from the source of Courage. It will never fail us. We find it time and time again and lean on each other when the well of Courage is a bit dry. We lean on prayer, dancing and touching mother earth. We lean on each other's heart vibes. The embrace of our sisterhood's Courage is immeasurable. We hold each other's hand in silence; listening as the heart conveys its wisdom.

We encourage each other because sometimes we can't see clearly just how beautiful we are. Sometimes the best we can do might not seem brave or courageous. It may even appear weak to some; but when we come up against our walls of conflict, pain and sadness we find flickers of hope, tenacity, endurance and faith. We rest in the sunspots of time and light candles for each other. We listen intently to the wind and let nature speak to that very dear space in our heart. It whispers a steady *I love you*.

Courage holds us while we mend. Courage instills in us strength beyond our understanding. Courage is vulnerability turned inside out; our hearts are exposed. We find the beautiful colors of our soul in the darkest of places. It is a breaking down of old boundaries and giving breath to new. We find Courage and strength in the most difficult life stages. It's the seed of perseverance and the ability not to harden but to grow. We might at first shrink but then we expand and spill into the river of our heart's flow.

Courage is the water of our soul's garden. It feeds all our flowers, plants and even those ever abundant weeds. We need the full spectrum of life's difficulties to fully grow. It's an exponential process and the gift of Courage produces a delectable sunlight of empathy. We transverse through the seasons: shedding, dormant, budding and flourishing into an endless cycle of courageous ability to comprehend and produce the fruits of our brave, poetic souls.

Strength In Being Seen
by Victoria Erickson

I see you standing there with a mouthful of poetry
yet a head full of doubt.
You are sharp yet softening
while needing to be split open
and poured out.
So let go.
All the things you now carry
all weights that pull you down
all the beauty you'd forgotten
any flame burned out.
Tell me
what awaits just beyond
the edge
of your ache.
There's relief
in the speaking.
And there's strength
in being seen.

Why the Lotus Blooms
by Charu Agarwal

The seed was released;
alone herself she found;
Pitch heavy darkness
weighed down all around.

"Where, what, why…?"
bewildered, she cried.
After a short while,
gathering herself, she sighed

"There must be a purpose
to my being here

I have to believe
in time it will be clear"

Trembling all the while,
emerging from her shell,
she sent her roots down
to anchor in the bed.

Groping in dull waters,
she looked around confused,
relieved to see above her
a golden beam diffused.

Reaching for the shimmer,
she extended herself up,
trudging through the mire
without the slightest fuss.

She rose to the surface
by now a reticent bud
savoring the air,
stood tall above the mud.

Warm rays embraced her
and lovingly kissed her face;
She had made her way home
...with splendor & grace

Her joyous petals whispered...
"inspire them, tell your story"
so laying bare her heart...
she bloomed... in all her glory.

Night and Day
by Alise Versella

Speak, for you are from the storm
Let the thunder roll
And lightning crack
Don't let droplets of rainfall
Let all your burning tears pour
Let them flood the riverbanks
And breathe new life to the world
Let your voice be heard
Bang mighty Neptune's sword
Let the lava erupt from the core
No soft breeze shall cool their ears
Let them feel the burning rays of day…
…Desire said to take the night
And hold it to your breast
Don't be gentle; have your way
Take what's yours, my dear
You deserve the stars and moonlight
You were born from a cruel midnight
Whisper the lies they raised you on
Then take their beating hearts
And leave this night empty
A void
An abyss where a world once dwelled.

Fire
by Jackie VanCampen

Fire rising from my soul
Burning through the veils of fear
Bringing to ashes the walls of my confinement
Freeing me from the shackles of suffering

Fire that consumes my past—
That dictates where I should be

Fire that licks and destroys
The anguish within me
Liberating my heart and opening my path

Fire that dances all around me
In perfect rhythm and movement
Hypnotizing my mind and moving my body
In balanced harmony
Arousing the lioness strength
Within my heart

Fire that strengthens my calling
That leads me to my newness
Ignites my passion
And gives rise to the wise woman within—Kahlia

Fire, oh great fire
Of ancient times
Burn my soul
With your powerful flames

I walk through you
United with your light
I emerge on the other side
Skin intact
Heart aflame
Like a torch
That sets fire to fields
Burning down any remaining limitation—
Of beliefs that hold me back

I find in you my gentle voice
And yet, resounding sound
That neither frightens or is meek
It empowers and awakens
That which must crack open
In order to seed and bloom
Cleansing my soul

Purifying my senses
Bringing me to my explosion
Shattering me to pieces
Just to bring me back to my wholeness.

Learning to Say No
by Krista Katrovas

I celebrate my ability to say NO.
I celebrate myself
When I say NO.
NO, to anyone
Who calls me names that hurt my heart.
NO, to anyone,
Who disrespects my need to honor myself.
NO, to anyone who abuses,
My kindness, my sensitivity, my generosity,
My wobbly knees
Learning to Say, No,
When I practice Self Love.
I celebrate myself,
Leaving the girl behind
Who was shamed when she said, NO.
The girl who was not taught,
But then later learned on her own,
That saying No,
Is also connected
As a partner in dance,
Gliding in perfect balance,
With YES!

Sky and Cage
by BethAnne Kapansky

You owe yourself to no one.

Your precious energy
your life force indebted
to none but you as you
find and live your heart path.

Along the way you may find
you share freely and willingly
with others whose paths you
cross in beautiful, woven
harmonious connection.

But your lovely breaths
are not meant to be bound
or obligated, only given
by choice and open heart.

This is the difference between
freedom and enslavement
love and imitation
grace and law,
Sky and cage.

I'm Not Afraid
by Jackie VanCampen

I'm not afraid
To enter the darkness of my soul
I'm not afraid
Of my soul's desire for freedom
I'm not afraid
To explore the dark parts of myself
I'm not afraid

Of my passion
My desires
My fire
My womanhood
The Priestess Goddess within me

I'm not afraid
To lose myself
When I know that I'm going to find myself
I'm not afraid
To lose control
When I know that
Control is of the ego
I'm not afraid
Of my passion
My desires
My womanhood
The Feminine Warrior within me

I'm not afraid
Of my intensity
When I know that
It's my intensity that
Helps me be who I am - to the fullest
I'm not afraid
To step into my power
When I know that
Power is the vehicle that
Helps me to be who I am - to the fullest
I'm not afraid
Of my passion
My desires
My womanhood
The Gentle Queen within me

I'm not afraid
Of my dark womb
When I know that

It's my womb that
Nourishes and delivers me
I'm not afraid
To die
When I know that
Death is the portal to life
I'm not afraid
To open my heart
When I know that
My heart is the portal to love
I'm not afraid
Of my passion
My desires
My womanhood
The Compassionate Leader within me

I'm not afraid of
Exploring my desires
Discovering my passion
Honoring my womanhood
Bringing forth the light within me.

Flying into Nothingness
by Alice Maldonado Gallardo

When you shine your light
you also show
your position
to the enemy
in the battlefield.
Shine anyway.
Blind them
with your light.

There is reason
to this madness.

Devour the strength
within you,
feed and nourish
your Self.
Then expand your wings
and keep flying straight.
Let your wings
strike each corner
of reality.
Let the air
breeze in,
elevating you
even higher.
Shatter mercilessly
the imaginary boundaries.
Lacerate all bondage.

There is power
in this madness.

Let the strong beat
of your heart
face
the approaching
war drums.
Let yourself
be born
again
and again.
Explode
as a star
being born
in the fullness
of the void
inside
and outside
the universe.

You are
one
and you are
all.

Increase your crescendo
in the Master's
symphony.
Leave them deaf.

Be more than brave.
Embrace yourself,
and fly
into
Nothingness.

Holding on to Letting Go
by Darshana Mahtani

Today I was given a lifetime opportunity.
I was asked to let go
Of all the things I don't want,
I don't need.
To write them on paper, at least.
To throw them in the crucible
To burn them...
From within.
It's hard to come to terms
With the things you hold on to
That no longer serve you.
Where to start?
My fears,
My doubts,
My insecurities.
My constant need for acceptance and approval,
Associating my worth to my body,
Feeling like I don't fit the standard definition of "pretty",

My mistakes, my flaws, my faults
My guilt,
My expectations.
"Let them go" a little voice whispered to me.
Let them go and live from your soul.
Allow yourself to be.
That beautiful, wonderful being that you are
That perfection in you
Because that's what you are.
You are perfect.
You're the reason
the definition of the word perfect even exists,
because there is nothing perfect in this world
yet we know what it is.
Listen to your heart.
Let it go…
Everything you think you are,
Everything you think you know,
And just breathe.
Just be.
Because in that being,
Dwells a divine masterpiece.

Who Shushed your Shouts?
by Anita Grace Brown

where are your sighs stuffed?
might they be lodged
in locked chamber
anticipating the day of their groaning

lamenting leaves
fluttered on boughs
discerning
the benefits of
coming unhinged,
drifting upward

glance around—
the scarlet Oaks' leafed limbs
flurry in their freedom
lyrically unfettered
gusted by wind on moonlit ride

not cinched to sentiment
upon where to settle,
only flitting
on air beneath
like a ballad breath
whooshing

stoic lantern
nearly still, in its long-suffering
caused an outrage
in the wood

just joggle!!
let the inner tempest
loose you

whistle your murmurs
howl your deplorable lamenting

you have shouts
that require visceral absolution!!
release them to the silvery wind
carried afar
on the current of life

what awaited
after the shouts and the sighs
made their goodbyes
was a marvelous
strain
a flurry drifting, vibrating o'er
the reed

emptied of drivel
what remained?
a hymn-like prayer,
notes innately
caressing
flowing
flowering
a symphonic
aria smile
bubbling up,
effervescent.

I Can
by Heather Awad

I can look up at a blue sky
like it's here just for me
on a day when gray clouds
would have pulled me
into the ground, the way
the earth drinks the rain.

I can write my emotions
in a poem till I've emptied
myself, less weighty, less
dispirited over another
estranged someone I gave
my heart to and had to
take it back.

I can wake up tomorrow
and it will be the next day
farther from this one
full of intrinsic belief
that the sky inside my heart
will be blue no matter what.

Falling Softly
by Romana Anna Nova

Although blindfolded
I am not afraid to make a step in the dark.
The voice inside
will guide me safely,
like no sight ever could
cut through the illusion.

The sharp edges which
make my eyes and feet bleed,
can't hurt me anymore,
because I'm letting go of all the peripherals.
What is unnecessary
will be severed.

The blades still cut.
My eyes and feet bleed as I walk,
but it doesn't hurt.
I let go of what is to go.
I let the blood drain,
and that's what keeps me alive,
because I no longer
resist the edges that
are there to shape me.

Surprised how little I need.
A narrow edge,
and nothing to hold on to,
is proving to be the safest haven,
where nothing can be lost,
nothing regretted.

Only the experience matters
of falling slowly
trusting
that there is no bottom to the void.

Somehow the mere force of gravity
strips away all that is arbitrary
and distills my essence—
the hard core
so light
that nothing
can touch it.

SHE
by MaRa LuaSa

I Am She Who Dreams;
Who Plants the seeds,
Of Eternal Promise,
Hopes and Visions of Whole-y Lands;
Unified Hearts and abundant light.

I Am She Who Dreams;
The Dances of Creation,
In Rhythmic One-Time of the heart;
Twirling, Swirling, Rapturous Rituals
That step in time with Gaia's Pulse.

I Am She Who Dreams;
Of love so deep,
It shatters illusions,
That have shackled the heart,
And pushes the breath of life,
Into the places that were un-lived.

I Am She Who Dreams;
The foundations of our children's future;
Who lays the stones-the sacred bones- upon the earth,
Of future temples,
Where sacred love,
Join hearts as ONE.

I Am She Who Dreams,
And Awakens the Heart,
Within and Without,
Of A New World,
A Unified Collective Harmonic;
Where Miracles are manifest in every moment
And every being lives in the Wholeness of the One Heart.
I Am She Whose Dreams Be-Come a Reality.

7

Voicing Soul Secrets

"Wild moon woman, you were not made to be tame.
You are an earthquake shaking loose everything
that is not soul.
Shake, woman, shake."

Elyse Morgan

A Dance with Oneness
by Tammy T. Stone

A secret rises to our lips, beguiling and unnamable, lush and mysterious, alive with the potential to liberate us in a beautiful act of revelation.

One of the most special qualities we possess as humans is that we can explore the hidden and bring it to light; we can know the illumined from the shadowed, and we can seek out those deepest secrets without and within. These are the secrets of nature and the cosmos, which are only obscured from us as long as we have not yet found our pathway there.

These are the secrets and truths of our very own souls, and we have the power to bring them into the fiery brightness of day.

It is our birthright to dive with full abandon into the life we have been given, and to thrive amid the most intimate communions, where secrets have no need for conception. Yet in many ways, we are still a world divided, and so secrets are made, and forged deep within our crevasses, along the fabric of our collective being.

Perhaps our secrets originate in forces of suppression vast and deep, or maybe we've been taught to believe that we are not free to acknowledge and express what blooms within. We may have come to take this as Truth, and found ways to live around the promise of our souls' deepest wishes.

But then, the time comes when a burning need overtakes, a calling, and we are humbled and ecstatic before the urge to lay our secrets bare, so that they transform into beautiful manifestations of the fierce uniqueness of our being. We discover that secrets burn holes where wholeness should dwell. We find the words to convey the reservoir of creativity we've been harboring since the beginning of all there is.

The unleashing of our souls' secrets is nothing less than an act of divinity coursing through us, a dance with sparkling oneness within pristine and eternal Time, as we find true homes in our bodies, on earth and beyond.

Who among us doesn't walk the earth with the songs of our souls waiting to emerge? And so we carve a space for silence, and we remember what has been forgotten. We surrender so that enchantment may come. We take refuge in Mother Earth, under the moon, in the stars above. We revel before the sun as it casts its last embers of day, in the bud of a seed bursting into new life, in the ineffable moments of life that flow within us like cosmic breath. The mysteries do not only inspire questions, but penetrate on levels we cannot glimpse with our conscious minds; they hint to us in our dreams, and gently evoke our expressive powers.

With this, our gift of expression, we hold space for the dreams and stories our soul secrets reveal, and awaken as a life unified and divine.

May these beautiful poems voicing soul secrets illumine us all!

Look Within
by Jasmine Kang

The face is changing in the mirror.
What was one day is not today.
What does one see?
Is there more to the face than what is seen?
Do you believe?
Belief comes from the heart.

The heart yearns for the universal Truth.
An ocean breeze caresses me.
The spirit sings in me, and dances to the tune
That rings against my heart.
Every day is a guide into the self.
It's like a song: a forever-unending song.

It's like when the wind blows again and again
As if someone's calling you,
And you feel something
Like a raindrop that falls
And touches your soul,
And everything changes.

You want to fly away,
You want to be free,
But freedom is not there.
It is already here.
You only have to look within,
And you will be flying.

Life is such a mystery, profound and deep,
Like the depths of the oceans and the seas.
Even in nothing, there is something.
If only you could look inside and see.
This is your home,
The temple of everlasting love and light.

Even if you're lost and lose the way,
You're not alone. You never were. You never will be.
We are all wanderers in the Whole on this journey.
We are all looking and searching for a way.
We can all find the way back where we belong.
Wherever you are, wherever you're going, just look within.

I AM
by Jamie Burgess

I am a smile from a kind stranger
at the end of the day.
I am the contagiousness of laughing children,
a reminder to live while still alive.
I am warm sunlight
washing over the darkness.
I am the heart
softening.
I am breath.
I am flame.
I am silence.
I am the fullness of the moon
on a black night.
I am
rising.

Sutra of Stars
by Taya Malakian

There is a web that weaves
the fabric of creation together

in a net that contracts and expands.

Eons pass with each inhale and each exhale.

From the tiniest fiber

to the whole of the infinite Universes,
there is no separation from the rhythmic dance
of creation.

There is a Sutra of Stars
that draws the heavens together in its spiral.

There is an orchestra amongst the atoms
so that even the most miniscule
is a seed of the profound.

The countless threads that spin
through every moment, every particle
like beads of a necklace,

pearls on a web.

Each strand stimulating the others,

in a cosmic cascade of energy.

The journey from here to the farthest reaches
would take you right back to where you began.

If you pluck just one string
they all will vibrate
with the same song.

The Wind of the Soul
by Nancy Carlson

Surrounded by quiet
a feeling of space
time seems to stop
settling into
this expansiveness

noticing the chatter of the mind
yet hearing the sound
of another, a calling
speaking from a different place,
in a different way
feeling like home
from the heart
in this moment
a conversation with Truth
a softness, with clarity
are these messages from the Divine?
Secret words
that speak of our eternalness,
our essence
words that ride on the wind
of our Soul
listening to the words,
beyond the words
letting them speak
surrendering to the currents
allowing to be heard,
and seen
sharing without attachment
or cause
letting it all bubble up
and out
into the world
the wind of the Soul…poetry.

Upon the Riverbed of my Soul
by Charu Agarwal

Upon the riverbed of my soul
Life-currents clear me as they flow:
Dark crevices with secrets deep…
Breathe easy in their rolling sweep.

Upon the riverbed of my soul
Life-currents shape me as they flow:
Eroding facets of the self…
That think they're separate from all else.

Upon the riverbed of my soul
Life-currents teach me as they flow
And all they ask of me is this:
Just allow us—don't resist.

Soul Song
by Sandra Allagapen

In the hills of Assisi
My soul found me
DREAM, it said
And you shall find your power
GROW, it whispered
And you shall expand into Oneness.

In the hills of Assisi
My heart found me
LOVE, it said
And you shall find beauty in everything
FEEL, it whispered
And I will sing for you every day.

In the hills of Assisi
My spirit found me
CELEBRATE it said
And you will live in joy
LEAP it whispered
And you shall soar beyond the stars.

In the hills of Assisi
Life found me
SMILE, it said

For you are free
DANCE, it said
For you are eternal.

Alone Time
by Krista Katrovas

Alone time
is sacred time.
I feel the rhythm of my breath,
the pause residing between thoughts,
where everything slows down
and vibrant colors return.
I no longer live
in hues of black, gray,
and white.
I remember myself,
the self I've always known,
even as a child,
while in the peace
of my own company.
Sometimes she hides
behind the hustle, the bustle,
the busy, the grasping,
and it's sacred alone time
that brings her back out,
as if she hides behind a sycamore,
in nature, with my true nature,
holding the limbs
of the tree as hands
of friends
for comfort.
I beckon her out,
with silence, aloneness,
that is her, my, music.
When she dances,
it serves her, me, us

with opportunity
to simply be,
free,
and we become one,
no longer split, no longer separated
from ourselves.

Flying Free
by Charu Agarwal

Oh! How I wish
I could fly
Soar up
in the limitless sky
Feel the breeze
upon my wings
No care, no worry—
not a thing

My mind
Silenced
and in awe
Overwhelmed
by what it saw—
All of creation
in its majestic glory
would shatter the illusion
of my personal story

Vibrantly alive
enveloped in rapture
My spirit would rise
as its own Master
Then seeing on the horizon
The beckoning Sun
Ah! Finally…
I could merge and be One.

Silence, I am Yours
by Vrinda Aguilera

Silence, I am yours
You have my ear, my heart

Silence, I see you donned in your cloak of quietude
I notice the absence of ripples not stirred by you
I stroke your vast abyss which is by no means vacant
Your emptiness fills my heart for you are actually not empty, not at
  all

You are robust in your presence
Velvety and smooth and black as spent embers
Or the rich cocoa of a moonless night

Silence, a smile plays on my lips as we share an unheard joke
But I hear you and grasp your slight, oh so subtle wit

It is you and I, dancing into the night
Yours palms are never sweaty
I let you lead and am comforted by your tender sway

Silence I am yours.

The Covenant Within
by Sonja Marie Phillips-Hollie

Into this quiet place,
I fly
without wings
deep inside the catacombs
of my mind.
I find home
I find me
in this secret place
where thoughts are transformed,

where mortal and immortal merge
as I become love
and love becomes me.
I drift into a sense
 of belonging
on a journey of truth
and self discovery.
Some
may call this quiet place
a mystery,
a lucid dream.
But, I call it…
The true covenant
Of Goddess,
inside of me.

Reverence
by Andreja Cepus

In Love Divine I Live
And Mother Earth is pulsing in my Heart
Reverence to Life.
In Light I bathe my Mind
To hear Creator's Thoughts:
Pure, Crystal-clear, Divine,
Reverence to Life.
Venus and Sun
Together in Me
I watch their Love Dance
And I feel Reverence.

The Embrace: You and I
by Zahra Akbarzadeh

You're the embrace I rest in
Take me from me to become you

You're the kiss whose flame I light
Touch me in every cell of you

You're the fragrance of that rose I bloom
You're the garden of me, I'm the garden of you

You're the wine thirsty for the lips I am
Flow me in the vein of you

Who can separate me from you?
When you are me, I am you

No time, no space, nobody
All is all, all is me, all is you.

Master of the Heart
by Sitara Alaknanda Shakti

I was living separately
The Madman came and took me
He propelled me to such elevating heights
And dropped me to such bottomless depths
Then Genuine of the Soul
Spoke to me so loudly
My senses started to blur
And I could no longer be just a body
Before it all, there was the One Word
Before me, there is the One Word
I bow at the feet of the Only
And I follow It resolutely

I forsake the here and there
And find myself dwelling in the Great Void
So when I look into your eyes
I can honestly say I in the I
No longer an exodus from my own kind
The Master of the Heart finally came for me
Together we proclaim unity
Together we are the Divine's infinite potentiality.

8
Voicing Revelations

"Whatever happens to you belongs to you. Make it yours. Feed it to yourself even if it feels impossible to swallow. Let it nurture you, because it will."

Cheryl Strayed

Searching for the One, the We, the All

by Julie Prentice

The voices in this chapter describe powerful, often life-changing revelations. They capture moments of awe and gratitude in which we will at times seem to be part of a "divine or supernatural disclosure to humans of something relating to human existence in the world," or of deep and meaningful realizations that were not previously unknown to us. These two definitions fit the power of mystery and myth spoken of by the women in this chapter. With each poem another unveiling occurs, along with another opportunity to appreciate the significance of revelations in each of our lives.

In this volume of spiritual poetry, these revelations appear as individual searches for the divine, the Goddess, the one and all. The poets explore the truths that are discovered when undertaking that search, walking that path. The telling is of the stumbling, reaching and eventual attaining of truth and power.

The process can be painful but the rewards great indeed. We hear these poetic voices sometimes ringing out, and other times whispering of the unknown insights that await those who search for new ways of perceiving and experiencing the world.

Another way to define the experiences captured in the following poems is as experiences of delightful surprise. For revelations often arrive as surprises: a previously unknown that becomes known, or a secret that unfolds, bringing things into a new light. So these poems bring to light the hidden and unknown, shining a lantern of wisdom to illuminate our darkness. Whether exploring the 'universal cathedral' or searching for the thousand names of the holy, through reading these women's revelations we are drawn into the experience of surprise and wonder as new spirituality opens like a blossom. Growing, exuding beauty and intoxicating aroma, the words lead us to a representation of the element of shock in knowing something for the first time that is paradoxically felt as both old and new.

...d Glass Heart
...n Riker

...fell
... of stained glass

she gathered each colorful slice
and laid out an abstract configuration

forgoing the obvious
and letting the rules slip away

she gathered strength from *knowing*
and ignored the critics.

she snipped the tattered stitches from brokenness
and let fresh chords play harmony into the spaces

she stood in the thickest part of her
heart and rearranged her perspective.

closing her eyes,
she let nature naturally speak,

what you are, is beautiful
your wings are boundless
a semi-circle of luminescence
let your voice be heard

her vision expanded
into an arching opalescent aura

and as she opened her eyes she
could clearly see

through a brilliant stained glass window

etched in her heart and the words:

It takes time to create a masterpiece.

Be Coming
by Kai Coggin

Hold all my aching and growing,
make your body a vessel
for everything I have to fill you,
it may not be much
but it might just be everything.

I have heard the soul is shaped like a bowl
a reversed dome of the Heavens,
we are golden receptors of beauty,
magnets that pull stars into our lowest points
until they build towers of light
from our sternums.

Rise and fall chest,
metronomic movement of body
keeping time for the sages,
inside me a heart breathing
sound of lullabies for sleeping angels,
Great Servers
who wear gravity like a badge of honor,
like a gown of trees rooted in earth,

wake up, my friends,
hold my hand through this;
I think I know the way,
otherwise, my true north tongue
will hasten into Mercury-mouthed
stutters of half truths
and I will taste the metal compass spin,
follow my fallen sparred-off feathers

to the gates of your own becoming,
Be coming,
Be going back to that body of light
that birthed you like a sun into space,
the plasma of dreams,
the expectancy of orbits,
the nomenclature of God, who has a thousand names

All of them being You.
All of them being Me.

The Season of Truth
by Alice Maldonado Gallardo

There is a season
between Autumn and Winter
when there are no secrets.
The trees are naked.
The forests are vulnerable.
Your eyes can find
all the little scars,
fragile branches,
and hidden nests
left behind
by life itself.
The structures of man
are no match
to those of
Mother Nature.
Even the highest
church tower
reaching for the sky
could never
capture heaven
as the stillness of the lake
mirrors its perfection.
Divine symmetry

of all the senses.
A complete circle
now exposed
by the light of the
distant sun.
This is the season
of showing
the roots
of all.

Experience
by Jasmine Kang

Today, tomorrow, and there lies yesterday.
Like a dream, it came,
And like a dream, it goes.
She sat and thought as the light touched her.

I am the watcher.
Life is you and what you make it to be.
We sight stars, and it is passion that holds us strong.
Touch the sun and moon in heaven, and reach for the skies.

The story weaver spins her yarns on her spinning wheel.
There are tales to create and recount.
One yarn after another is spun.
Every color of the spectrum becomes One.

As the hour glass of time slowly pushes its sand to the bottom
With it changes time as the midnight blue of dusk awakens to dawn,
But the sand stays all the same.
So, we come in many forms, but we are the One and the Same.

She weaves in her reveries,
And listens to what nature has to tell her.

Every song has a tale woven within it.
Every form in life has its own story to tell.

Before me lies a future,
And behind me there is a past.
Infinite are these forms of nature
And the memories we have etched.

There is something to remember and something to forget.
There are days filled with reminiscences of the past long gone.
The future draws nearer as each moment slips away incessantly.
There is a moment to be lived: it is now.

Images of the past came to her mind,
And her future dawned upon her.
She felt the light again and remembered:
"Live in the present moment."

Look before you, and you will recognize the vastness of the
　　Universe.
It lies before one like a tableau within a frame.
Become a part of it, and one is caught in its colorful drama.
This is the experience of life.

Listen to the songbirds,
Feel the rhythm, and breathe.
You realize there is more to life
Than what you see and perceive to be.

There is a blessing in every moment,
A bit of it in everyone and everything.
So vast and so deep,
The Light within you embodies all of life.

She Believed
by Carolyn Riker

Sunny rays of amber and gold

sifted through her lashes

She believed in love
held onto the wisps
and felt the stir of moonlight shifts

As the years prevailed
tattered, twisted and trivialized
perceptions were altered

Her free-spirit, turned to ebony fragments
weather-worn, chastised and achy

The illusion of love was deeply torn
the silver lining was tarnished and forlorn

And into the safety of her shadows

she dipped deeper,
until a passion to live released her

She would no longer conform.
Or bend to the point of breaking
She set her creative intuition free

She accepted her soul as a dreamer
one foot in this world
another in a rapturous sea

Love didn't lose its luster
because love is a mixture of spirit and nature
It is the divine found in you and me.

I Am Free
by Anjuu Kalhaan

I am free.
Free is my soul.
Free is my mind.
Why bind it with the past?
Why think about the future?
The moment I spend with myself is the freedom that I seek.

Free is my spirit
Free is my thought.
Why bind it in the past?
Why think about the future?
The breath I inhale is my life and I have plenty left to breathe.

Free is my heart
Free is my body
Why bind it in the past?
Why think about the future?
The walk I tread is towards eternity and that is what embraces me.

Earth is where I stand and heaven is my ceiling.
I return Life's embrace when I fly and feel life thriving within me.
Free is my soul
Free is my mind.
I am free!

The Things I've Built
by Alise Versella

I took a pencil to an all blank page to create a world I was in control of
It went from sketchy shadows to bolder lines the stronger I became
I knew what I wanted would not proceed to fall into my lap
So I reached passed those who stood in my way
To take whatever it was that I could grab

I created words that conveyed how I felt
And I didn't care who they'd offend
I spoke from where the seas had swelled
Wreaking havoc on the shores
Of all those countries who denied me entry
I raged like nature at her worst
And nonetheless felt no shame nor guilt
I finished the fortress I had long dreamt to build.
I was powerful in my beauty
And others ran
For I refused to be an object
To be held and contained
I couldn't let them in
For they lied
In hopes of grasping a ghost of a girl
Who ran faster than they could run
Unable to catch up
I left the weak and weary behind.
I chose to turn the leaves over in their mud
So I could become something better
And when I returned you would be in awe
Of the girl you never called
She'd sit higher up on a pedestal
So high you couldn't reach
And my voice would ring out louder and stronger
Than any voice could ever preach
Some days I feel like everything I'd drawn
Should be done over, erased
But then I look at how far I've gotten
And how much I wouldn't give it up
For everything it's taken me
To get passed where I've gone
Nothing you could've given me would make me ever give this up.
For all you thought I lacked
I'd like to have all I gave you back
To safeguard it in my fortress behind my ever sturdy walls
While you sit back and wonder how

All you created crumbled and fell
I'll be ever still creating a world that burns brighter than the sun
And I'll be forever running until there's no place left for me to go.

The Cheetah
by Abra Duprea

Imbibing the duskened light
of a slowly sinking sun,
these blades of grass, tall and thin,
become pale green waves in the breeze.
I feel them glide across my cheek,
as I run, effortless and free.

The air is warm, the dirt is soft;
the fields are alive and thriving.
Where shall I go today?
What shall I see?

The winds are my compass
and like them, I am wild;
a shooting star making its way
across an impressive sky.
What will be, will be.

I have returned to this land,
to this home I once dreamed,
all those years and not so many ago.

With the taste of veritable peace upon my lips.
Where shall I go today?
What shall I see?

Inner Mystery
by Sonja Marie Phillips-Hollie

There is a divinity
inside of me,
that no eye can see.
She is called Love,
Wisdom and Mystery.
And all that I Am, is She.
within her Providence,
lies the universal cathedral
in a mystery.
and deep within her crown lies the sacred energy.
There is a divinity inside of me,
an image no eye can see.
she is called deception,
darkness and iniquity!
her fragrance is duality.
At last,
I too must embrace her
All that is She.
Because all that I am, is She.

Words, Lovely Words
by Louise Marcotte Desrosiers

words expressed
with meaningful intention—
lovely words,
were gifted to me…
at the chrysalis
of this opening of hearts
energies are flowing—
finding the need
to sit-breathe-
take it to my soul
my spirit intense…

"can this be real?"
to feel such luminosity
within me
within these moments
feeling so much joy...
"is this a dream?"
if so, allow me to continue
this lucid dreamtime:
hearing, feeling
moving gently into
unbroken moments
in its gradual unfolding,
simply, without confusion—
within its own divine time
until it's completely free to fly...

Listening to My Inner Voice
by Carolyn Riker

I let you into my heart:
a secret, sacred space.

My trust in you was assuredly there.
I prayed, it wouldn't be misused.

I gave pearls of veracity:
melodiously wrapped within my quiet self.

We were parallel lines drifting:
no longer converging but repelling
my synergy fully depleted.

I could give no more, knowing
superficial corrodes my intuitive helm.

My soul lamented, until I finally understood...

I must navigate the depths of the stars, land and sea.
My time had come to return to my dreams and be me.

Awareness
by Tracie Nichols

Awareness...

is wings
is needles of rain on my arm
is opening

o p e n i n g

o p e n i n g

eyes and mouths
hands and lungs

uncurling toes and
unclenching teeth

awareness

is droplets of my soul
scattered wherever
I go
wherever
I
am

glimmering
on sidewalks
in tree leaves
on blades of grass
becoming snowflakes

droplets of my soul
kissing
everything
at once

awareness
is taking
the
world
as my
lover.

Meeting
By Ruth Calder Murphy

Where pen and paper meet
—or Sound and Silence,
Day and Night,
the trespassing of the Word into the Void,
the tentative touching of Darkness and Light.

In the seams and horizons,
the fragile in-betweens,
in the thin places where nothing's as it seems;
where veils hang
and portals call
—where magic wreathes…
The places where Morpheus lives and breathes.

Where souls and spirits recognize
kindred light in one another's eyes
and memories from eons past and gone
join hearts and hands and histories
with things that are not, yet—
at the junctions where mysteries are met.

Where planets pulse and galaxies beat,
where the dancing feet and the distant drum
of everything that was and is and is to come,
echo in art and poetry
and the music that stirs somewhere deep in me
and my soul is lifted high on the sunrise sky
or whispers, low, the almost-forgotten wisdom of long ago…

Here, the heart of Divinity meets in me —
in the inhale and exhale
of Creativity.

9

Voicing Struggle

"For a seed to achieve its greatest expression, it must come completely undone. The shell cracks, its insides come out and everything changes. To someone who doesn't understand growth, it would look like complete destruction."
Cynthia Occelli

Planting Our Staff

by Tracie Nichols

Struggle, to me, has always seemed to describe something valiant, but likely doomed. There's a hardscrabble feel to the word. Heroic striving draped in overtones of fatigued futility. So when I volunteered to write the introduction to this Voicing Struggle chapter of poems, I was expecting the poems to mirror my assumptions about the word.

I couldn't have been more wrong: Tucked away in these poetic offerings were passages illustrating strength, courage, movement, progress, flow and expansive grace. I was flummoxed. Edged off kilter into a struggle with writing this introduction because the version I'd already written in my head now made no sense.

At least the irony of struggling with writing an introduction to a chapter full of poems on voicing struggle kept me smiling. But, I still needed to write something that honored both topic and poets. So, snuggled up against the deadline, still floundering, I started to reread each poem. Only this time I declaimed them, in full ringing voice, while standing with my feet firmly planted on the earth, back firmly planted to an old oak tree friend.

And the answer—their answer—flowed up through my rooted feet and broke dawn across my bogged brain: *Follow the poems!* Let them be the footsteps that make the journey of this introduction. From this insight, a poem of sorts emerged: Every stanza a quote from each of the thirteen poems in this chapter.

"I forgot my own name once,
I tucked it underneath the ledge of someone's grief,
and slept for a hundred years."

"I built a fence around myself
and painted it with tar...."

*"And I felt all the storms that you hide so well,
With your smile."*

"But do I dare release this fragile thing?"

*"Sometimes I feel
I sleep beneath
the mountain of my prayers."*

"Everything I thought I was is dissolving inside me."

"My entire life is unfolding in you."

*"I want
to forget that nothing goes unchanged
or becomes unhinged at the core."*

"I know I should trust...."

*"I'd just quit talking and
get right to the
doing."*

*" 'She be but little, but she is fierce'
The townspeople will say,
And even if they don't
Your heart knows it...."*

*"I lift the veil
of in-between-ness
and sigh into my ribs...."*

*"I surrendered.
A lovely heap of tears in child's pose, bowing to what is.
I have come back home."*

My felt understanding of struggle has been terraformed through the process of writing these 500 words. After living with the poems for weeks, after absorbing them into my very bones, it's not simply the way I understand the word struggle that has changed. I am changed. The terrain of my struggles has become less daunting. I'm seeing their strength and grace more clearly.

In this chapter, thirteen women have spoken. Thirteen voices have claimed engaged presence as their definition of struggle. Struggle, as these poets have illuminated it means "I am engaged. I am present. I am finding my way. I am raising my voice. I have come back home."

Fence
by Ruth Calder Murphy

I built a fence around myself
and painted it with tar,
attached a roof with just one space
through which I'd see one star
that rose to view at midnight,
and peeped into my box
and wondered at its smallness,
sealed up with bolts and locks.
One night, the star called out to me
down, from its midnight sky,
to join the great celestial dance,
to free myself and fly.
I frowned and said I couldn't,
incarcerated so—
how could I break the locks and bolts
and just decide to go?
The star, it twinkled violently,
and pointed out the truth:
that I, myself, had built the fence,
and I attached the roof.
The walls and doors and locks and bolts,
though surely very strong,
were on the inside, with the key—
and had been, all along.
At any moment, I could leave;
I only had to choose
to stand and slide the locks aside—
what had I got to lose?
I stood and stretched and looked around
and knew the time was right.
The locks clicked up, the bolts flew back,
I stepped into the night.
The Earth was wide and high and deep,
the stars burned bright and free

and there between, a dancing mote:
Emancipated Me.

Prisons
by Sarah Courtney Dean

My world is reduced to a prisoners view
From a glass caged window
Looking out while life goes on.
There are no bars or chains in this prison
Except those made from failing flesh.
But whilst flesh and blood fail
The world of the mind is set free
To soar past the confines of freshly concerns
Set free to roam
But do I dare to release this fragile thing
Much more delicate than the cage of flesh and blood
That confines it.
Dare I raise my hand and smash the glass cage
And in that act of violence set free my mind
Reflected in the shards of broken fun fair mirrors?

I forgot my name
by Kai Coggin

I forgot my own name once,
swallowed the aching words of so many women
that they became a dishcloth
lodged in my throat,
a muffle to my own mouth sounds,
and I was quick to judge myself,
unusual introversion,
what's wrong with me?
I'm not usually like this,
so inside,
so quiet,

a thrush blending into wood shadow,
conversations on repeat in my mind,
preventing my voice from finding the wet of night,
this much energy is not always a good thing,
being this sensitive, it hurts,
these eyes, these eyes
that see what everyone needs at all times,
these hands, these hands that only want to hold together
what is broken,
this heart, this heart that knows
too much is broken here,
this is a collection of sadness,
a gathering of shards under one fireside night, and
suddenly I forget my name,
because suddenly, I am all of them,
I am the anxieties,
I am the self-harm,
I am the dark blue thoughts,
I am broken legs and the bruised arms,
I am the depression,
I am the genderless shell of small child,
I am the abused,
I am the tears, and the shame and the loveless game
rampant in this cluster of women,
too much pain in one place, and my spark is a diminishing flicker,
oh soul,
where is my light?
oh soul,
what is my name?
I forgot my own name once,
I tucked it underneath the ledge of someone's grief,
and slept for a hundred years.
Before the birds woke, I sang of morning,
I found my name in the trees,
my three letters carved on trunk belly,
K A I,
I found my name in the sunrise
blanket warmth of daybreak,

s K A I, sky,
breathe periwinkle rise,
I found my name
under the leaves of a century-old willow,
the way the light shone through the magical fronds,
the swayback bends of the branches
bringing me back to the center of my self,
the vibrations of earth, and green, and peace, and calm
whispered,
"You are here and everywhere, Kai.
You are here and everywhere."

Flower
by Brigid Clare Oak

You call me into
this quiet space
where You alone
can teach me
You, of the Soft Hands
and the Tender Heart
You, of the Fierce Freedom
and Powerful Protection

You reach into
my woundedness
and draw me forth
from my own clutching keeping
Out of that tiny, hidden room
where the child is still weeping

You gather the vapor
from all around me
of what I have so carelessly given away
and from it, form a cloud
of cleansing rain above my head
to wash away all fear and dread

with Your kind, insistent shower—
to clear the dust of my diminishment
and reveal the gift of gracious power
You have bestowed upon me

Sometimes I feel
I sleep beneath
the mountain of my prayers
My light reluctant and resting underground
Oh…I have found treasure there
in the dark deep necessity of my hiding;
a Faithful Presence there abiding
while I so busy about mothering and othering
I did not notice I was smothering
in a cold cave of my own making

But once again
You are quaking
in my simple soul
So invested You are
in ushering me into the Light
and kissing me Whole—
in healing me and vesting me
in Your Own colorful finery—

a flower in Your Field,
face upturned to the Sun.

Lost November Days
by Salyna Gracie

Those barren days,
Last summer
I heard your insistent call

Over and over
Through the dry-scented pine

Frantic with expectation

And you,
In patient repose
Waiting,
Confident I would rise to the task

Finding you,
Shattered my glass heart
I cradled your darkness
Clutched at your stillness
A heaving, terrible beauty

I have known
For some time
That this is the season
For letting go

Yet, my hands lay idle
Folded on aching breast

I know I should trust
I know that your treasure
Lies not in these feathers
But, in the spirit that
Lifts them into flight

These could be happy tears.

Heart Roar
by Bryonie Wise

Sometimes,
I doubt the courage
My bones are made of

And then,
A breath finds her way in
And her way out

The half-way-almost-full-moon
Smiles down;

My heart sighs
And quietly whispers:
I remember.

Exploding Sun
by Gwen Potts

Emotions so real, so raw
Self-realization, a double-edged sword
Duality all around me, two sides of the same coin....
Through deeply feeling our pain
Can we come to find our deepest peace?

An expanded awareness that travels from other dimensions
The longest of journeys
Through time
Through space
The material and ethereal
All must be embraced, as to know one is to know the other
I cannot escape these thoughts and feelings
So real, so raw
No matter where I go or how far I travel
Whatever I experience or with whom I meet

I cannot deny myself

My conditioning, the distortions I carry
bubble up and out of me with the fullness of my soul
Feelings of not being good enough haunt my dreams and disturb
    my heart by day
How to accept this world with its pain and suffering?

I sense a reality so different from this separation I feel
As if from a distant memory of another lifetime
Where there is no illusion to confuse the heart
Where we dance in completeness
As radiant as a thousand suns!

Did I arrive here too early?
Frustration surfaces with what I see and feel around me
Is this reality?
How to accept this world yet at the same time
Hold the energy for a new earth to form?
Where we live in harmony — As One

The Earth is so beautiful
I am filled with wonder at nature's awesome splendor
Yet my heart cries at its destruction
I feel the pain as my own
Invoking deep sadness and a longing within
Inner peace
Just a dream?

I sense restlessness within my being, impatience…
I have gathered much knowledge along this path
Now, it's as if all I have ever learnt is exploding
Into nothingness before my eyes
I wish to follow no-one, no guru, no method, no teacher,
no dogma, no concepts
Just to stand strongly in my own deepest truth
Be my own guide
No system
No control

Just my own light illuminating each step on the path
Unfolding and ever changing

I wish to feel every part of myself
Raw and naked to the world
Letting go of fear

So that someday I will explode into a thousand pieces
My pain a catalyst that turns the hungry caterpillar
Into the humble butterfly

Though in this moment I cannot hold any particular form
No concept
I have no clue of who I am becoming
I have no energy to hold any particular outcome
All I am left with are feelings
No past and no future
Growing weary of efforting at all
Everything I thought I was is dissolving inside me
I can hold nothing

Who am I becoming?
What is my purpose here?
I have no response

I am nothing and everything as one.

Disillusion
by Dana Gornall

I want
long summer nights that
stretch on for days and skies full of
falling stars that lead to wishes that
lead
to dreaming with my eyes open.

I want
a warm bed at night that
beckons me into sweet sound slumber
without thoughts from the day
filling
my head full of worries and insecurities.

I want
a pink sun in the morning that
turns the sky a rosy glow and promises
a fine day ahead full of happy
deeds
done with kindness from the heart.

I want
to unwind the hands of time so that I could
once again live in that space
of believing in the things deemed to be
impossible
and are in fact quite plausible.

I want
to forget that nothing goes unchanged
or becomes unhinged at the core
but people and things are actually
constant
reliable and invariable.

I want
those things that come from the places
in my mind when I am at the edge of sleep and wake
or wake and sleep, so much that I sometimes
forget
that's just
not how
it goes.

Breathing in Myself
by Rachelle Smith Stokes

Do mountains get tired?
Is that why they crumble or erupt
after standing strong for so long?

Or so it thought.
The top dumps off or its inside explodes.

I couldn't bear *tadasana* today.
Being still was too much
as I finally felt grounded beneath my feet.
Quiet and still I was alone.
Breathing in myself like a mountain.

I cried
Instead of sweat.
I folded swiftly to more earth
Instead of crumpling like somber rocks.
I became quiet and studied inward
Instead of bursting like angry lava.

My mountain didn't collapse.
I surrendered.
A lovely heap of tears in child's pose, bowing to what is.
I have come back home.
Earth, infant, weeping.
Wondering where it all came from.
Humbled
To begin once more.

Sit with me in the I don't know
by Anita Grace Brown

i don't know what the words mean
and i don't know
if they matter.
this is suddenly so shocking
i may just topple,
like a rooted Oak
recently struck
by a great bolt of lightning
and beginning its inevitable

descent.
into
what?
the earth of course,
where it first began its
journey to greatness
as an inconsequential
acorn, containing all the
instructions
for magnificence.
imagine
the end of communication
as we know it.
yet i feel so attached
to
those
words.
the ones that ring true in my spirit.
i love the way they roll off my tongue:
embody
delicious
serendipity.
my word is my bond
whatever that means…
but what if…
what if
what i really needed
was to release
the words and their
groaning.
to set the prisoners free!
to express my deepest feelings-
right from the pit
of
me.
i would not verbalize
any longer.
i'd just quit talking and

get right to the
doing.
i'd be left with
bear hugs
and divine gazes,
long, sultry kisses,
rich sighs and
toothy smiles.
pregnant pauses
filled with pure potential.
i'd be left with
breath:
fully inspirational inhales
emptying exhales
replete with surrender.
oh,
and
deep listening.
i'd be all ears.
because there's still a lot
i don't know.
and i can't possibly know
if i continue on
talking
and writing
writing
and talking.
won't you
sit with me?

One Day
by Yvonne Brewer

You never told me, but Little Boy did.
As you sang to the crowd he closed his eyes,
He fell into my arms and oh how he cried. He cried. He cried.
And I felt all the storms that you hide so well,

With your smile.

Hiding,
Like you always did, under your bed.
Humming and writing songs
Until, their arguing would end.
You wanted to sing it all away, but why does that lump still
    remain,
From all those tears you have stored for years
As you try to swallow all the pain.

But when you ran with the waves, built castles and
Played hide and seek in the caves,
Your tears were dried by the wind,
Bad memories were blown away in the sand.
And you could dream that today might be the day
She would smile and hold your hand.
Your Guardian Angels could reach you there and
Give you comfort, love and care.
Days of rest, Nights of sleep,
Sweet whispers in your ear "Her love will always keep"

Until then, I will carry Little Boy in my arms.
Warm him with every breath,
Wrap him in my heart.
Hum him a lullaby,
Make him a pie,

So that
One
Day,
You
Will
Know
Love,
Little Boy.

The Fierce One
by Eva Xanthopolus

It's a steep one, little (but *fierce*) one—
The hill yonder;
Much too steep for you,
so you best stay in the fields.

But, "No!" you say
"There are crests in the most
zest-emptied of places that need
climbing—that's the only way
to reach our dreams & stars!"

To many, you're just skin & bone,
Can't amount to much all on your own—
*Can't they see the kindred soul
& shakti* that beams beneath?*

The climb isn't what worries your
little legs, it's that big heart &
what happens to it during
the inevitable
descent.

There are African Violets, *fierce* one—
At the hill's other end;
The journey to them may be dangerous,
so you best stay in the fields where it's safe.

But, "No!" you say,
"There are prizes to be reaped by those
that trudge through the ups of life—
especially the downs of life without
downing the hemlock rum buried
'neath flora."

If go you must,
Then don't pick the flowers, fierce one—
Let your apatite* eyes see them & absorb
them into your vast memory banks. Allow
the prize to be their elegance.

At your next hill or Mount Everest,
No worries shall be…
"She be but little, but she is fierce"
The townspeople will say,
And even if they don't,
Your heart knows it,
knew it all along—
All women of every size,
nationality, shape
are graceful, exquisite
& ever-strong!

***Shakti** is the female principle of divine energy*
****Apatite** is a crystal and comes from the Greek word "to deceive." It may appear to be a beautiful, dainty rock… but it is very durable… Looks can be deceiving.*

I Sip Solitude
by Carolyn Riker

As the sun sets
I breathe peace
as the day ebbs into
the flow of eve
I find gratitude
in simplicity
I lift the veil
of in-between-ness
and sigh into my ribs
I feel the moss
shades of chartreuse

the day meets dusk
the color of hibiscus tea
I watch a dragonfly
tinted cobalt and emerald
and a pair of goldfinch
tenderly dance as I
sip solitude
and savory a
moment of
peace.

10
Voicing Prayers

"...It doesn't matter how you pray — with your head bowed in silence, or crying out in grief, or dancing. Churches are good for prayer, but so are garages and cars and mountains and showers and dance floors."

Anne Lamott

Heart Wishes

by Sandra Allagapen

A prayer is the expression of the soul reaching out to a Higher Power. Although we associate prayers mostly with requests for help, prayers can take many forms with the soul intention that the Divine hear them. So even with prayers that have been passed down throughout the ages, and repeated by millions all over the world, each time a prayer is recited it is as unique as the person saying it.

When you have reached the deep end and don't know where to turn, when you feel no one understands or is even listening to you, say a prayer. Ask for strength and to be guided to the people who can help you.

When you have lost the most important person in your life and don't want to imagine a future without them, say a prayer. Ask for comfort as you grieve and for peace until you meet again.

When you can't achieve your goals and feel ashamed, say a prayer. Ask for help and for compassion for yourself so you recognize that you are doing your best.

When you can't find what you are looking for and feel as if you don't belong anywhere, say a prayer. Ask for help so you may accept yourself and create that sense of home no matter where you are or whom you are with.

When you want your life to change but don't want to let go of what is, say a prayer. Ask for the courage to take that leap of faith.

When you have been hurt and cannot forgive, say a prayer. Ask for the strength to forgive others and yourself, just a little bit more each day.

When your loved ones are suffering and you feel helpless, say a prayer. Believe on their behalf and ask for their perfect care and health.

When you have no words to express what is in your heart, draw, dance or sing your sorrows. Surrender and let the Divine carry you for a short while as you empty your heavy heart. When you are ready, wake up and pay attention, for the answer to your prayers often comes from unexpected sources because there are no limits to miracles.

As children we are taught to say "Thank you" and we usually do when we are asking for something. But when a prayer is answered, we either forget or mumble a quickly forgotten "Thank You," thereby missing out on the blessings of the energy of gratitude, and its potential to create change in the world.

When your child makes you proud, let your heart fill with joy and send this as a blessing to all children and parents who are struggling. May their burden lift with the hope that soon they will be sharing the same joy.

When your loved one recovers, let gratitude fill every cell of your body and share it as a wish for others who are still in pain.

When you take that leap of faith and find yourself in a new world where you are valued and finally feel that you have found the place where you belong, let your heart sing the song of victory to the Universe and send out a prayer that anyone who is still fumbling in the dark, soon find their perfect places too.

When you come across a laughing child or a majestic mountain that takes your breath away, let your worries drop away if only for a moment, and pray that the peace that you are feeling is gifted to everyone who needs it.

When you finally see the light at the end of the tunnel, pray that others too, may be filled with hope.

When every challenge and joy that you encounter on this journey called Life, become reasons to reach out and connect with the Divine, your days will unfold like the most beautiful prayer.

I Am
by Shivana Sharma

I am my own soul
I am not the scream of the eagle
As he scrapes the sky
Though I scream at heaven
And hell too
I am the not the gust of stifling wind
That pushes hope to its knees
And blows ash into the eyes of the dreamer
I am not the lily
Nor the rose
There is no touch
No taste
No scent of beauty
I am not the proud noble mountain
I am the valley
The desert
The stone
I am not the spirit of the song
I am but one note
Quavering
Harsh
And softly sweet
I am the starless night sky
The thorn, the feather
The petal too
I am my soul
My smile
My tears
The black red blood
That joyously spills when I am quartered
I am the longing for the light that waits
On the other side
Of you
I am the certain dawn

I am tomorrow
I am my soul.

Praying
by Ruth Calder Murphy

When mist rises from the water
in-between night
and the golden light of dawn
- when it drifts,
translucent-white
or hangs like silent phantoms,
soaking up birdsong
and the perfume of honeysuckled hedgerows;
when herons launch themselves airborne
with a sudden decision and the precision of practice
and I run, Achilles-winged,
toes kissing the tow path
and beating the rhythm of another new day,
then, with every step
and every diaphragm-deep breath,
without the need for words,
I pray.

In Your Hands
by Alice Maldonado Gallardo

Nothing can extinguish your light
because you are in the center of the Sun.
No one can trample your flowers
because your garden is everlasting.

You are in the hands of God.
You are painfully immutable,
unreal and eternal.

The dove flies free
even inside the cage.
The water flows
even within the fist.
The air breathes
even trapped in the tomb.

Keep Flying,
Flowing,
Breathing.
You are in the hands of God.
You were never lost.

Yesterday,
Today,
Tomorrow,
in the hands of God.
And those hands
are made from prayers,
silences, laughter,
and love.

Remember your cradle,
return to your birth.
The memories are not yours,
they belong to God.
Only Love
carved in the hearts
remain.

Loneliness is the veil,
the fog imagined.
The mind seduces,
deceives,
abandons you.
But you do not
lose your place.

Do not go to sleep.
Stay awake.
The sun
always
shines best
at
midnight.

Fraught with Peace
by Anita Grace Brown

watershed tears
no reason and every
reason
clarity and confusion
share gray matter space
knitted together
the fibers marry
body sways and rocks
through cerulean gloom
yet
hope danced
and twirled
like a ballerina on tiptoe
above the rising pain
arms raised
releasing the world's anguish
one angry fist
one praise hand at a time
the heart speaks:
patience
slowly,
imperceptibly at first
resplendent light
lifts the dense
fog of mourn
immobility and helplessness
spiral into backbone

erect and courageous
peace
metamorphosized
like a monarch being beckoned
to life's garden
boldly, colorfully demonstrating.

Leaning Into the Ether
by Sally MacKinnon

There is a beach where the sound of the sea
speaks peace
Where the infinite sky remembers
and every grain of sand welcomes the feet, the paws, the claws, the
  life that press upon them.
That's where I join the tides and the sun
to craft patterns, rhythms, ephemeral shrines with my hands, feet,
  body, breath;
wondering if, in this most secular city
one can move energy in ways that conjure up cathedrals amongst
  the rocks.
Inhaling into pain, the resistance like a miracle
exhales in tandem and we dance
a tango I think,
unflinching
enamoured
elegant in hats and heels
Unflinching.
In our wake remain the whispers of devotion.
Until high tide they murmur, extending
petals, sticks, shells and pebbles within a ghostly
series of steps for passers-by with
an open eye.
After the last stretch I retreat to the big black boulder
press my back against its sun-drenched surface,
reflecting;
Akasha: I lean into the ether and sing.

Emergence
by Tammy T. Stone

The shrine of the tiny island forest
allows entry after hurtling gales of wind
onto the bridge, until the threshold is
crossed. The gods have been pacified by
our perseverance, and remark on our
long-awaited arrival, like they have been waiting.
Dried yellow leaves hang from the gate,
slick moss skirts along a log once reaching
for the low-hanging sky,
dewy but never cold.
I fall in the face of beauty every time.
I touch my forehead to Earth in reverence for its certainty.
The fall deepens, my thoughts absorbed
like they are the cherished secrets
I have hoped they'd become.
Every step, a new wondrous accounting
of the ground's ever-presence.
Wild life thrusts upward through
the obstacles we have made.
They will not be appeased,
they do not need our comfort.
The flower unfolding, in scarlet bloom,
never asking why, the tree's broad
leaves receiving.
I dream of a field where we can sit
and eat the light and drink the little river,
of sitting in the garden, where the sun fills
golden space.
Maybe it's true, that they've been
waiting these long years,
and now we've come.
The loveliness of clouds, white and suspended.
This is what the view wants to say:
I am you.
Steam rising over rocks,

a life force carved by love,
carrying the magic
of emergence.

Bridge Between Hearts
by Sandra Allagapen

The wind carries the echo of my name
A whisper to my awakening soul
Will I listen or will I evade in slumber
The purpose of my being?

The call resurrects a deep longing within
Before I can decide
My spirit soars and runs to the Source.

The journey takes me far away
Or is it deep within?
As I allow myself to float towards my destiny
I see other times with their pain and traumas.
Am I really going to do this again?
Have I not learned from the past?

Out of nowhere the answer springs forth
I am going to do this not in spite of the past
But because of it.
I have come too far and grown too much
To ignore this divine call

This truth lights my whole being with joy.
My purpose comes to life
I sing, I laugh, I cry
On the wings of faith I journey
Each step bringing me closer to wholeness.

I find myself in a forest
The green of which I have never seen

It lives and fills my senses with beauty
On a breath I wake up
Just like that.
I feel the source of life flow unhindered
In my blood, in my heart
I am alive.

I look around
Many others are already at work
My heart overflows with love
For magical they are
So much already done
So much more to come
Tirelessly they weave
The divine golden thread
Into the painting of life
With every touch, every word, every song.

In this circle my place I take
Honoured beyond words for I belong
In my heart a prayer
Lord, work with us, work through us.

Finally ready to listen, I hear:
This is the place you have been seeking
Where your human self meets your divine one
Heaven on Earth thus created
When consciously you live.

This is no place for illusions
In the clarity that shines
The Creator within you'll find
Together the Bridge of Love We'll build
For this is Our will.

A hiding place it is not
A sanctuary for your soul perhaps

where support, love and magic abound.
Remember, remember… sweet child
The truth of you… and soar
There has never been a better place than here
nor a better time than now

Sing, dance, laugh, love…
For in every song, step, smile and touch
I AM.

A Poem Without Words
by Taya Malakrain

I want to become a poem for the Beloved.

I want to set my pen aside
and give up the words
I have used to aim at my true lover.

With every aspect of my being,
I want to seduce the Divine.

Just like each moment
is filled with either sunshine,
or moonlight,
or darkness,
I want to fill myself with
whatever experience is being offered
and as a gift
reflect it back to my Beloved.

The delight of warm rain,
the silky cool of the mist that comes next,
the glow of the sun setting into the storm.

I want to take it all in
as you watch me experience it.

And instead of attempting
to capture all of this in words,
words that can only point
towards the truth,
I will become a poem for my Beloved.

Each aspect of my being a page on
which the Divine Poet
has written the most beautiful poem—
without using a single word.

Faith
by Vrinda Aguilera

Faith is a tiny, grey field mouse
Velvety pink nose sniffing, whiskers twitching
Foraging in a vast, flaxen field of wheat
Under a shaded, sheet metal sky

Faith is a weary farmer
Ploughing the fertile land
Bedding his seeds in the rich soil
With scarred, work roughened hands

Faith is a downy sparrow chick
Nestled in her forked branch treetop nest
Neck outstretched, blind eyes shut tight
Beak open wide in expectant anticipation

Faith is the golden sun descending
Leaving feathery streaks of pastel colors
Trailing artfully across the sky
Tipping the scales that send the moon on the rise

Faith is a tender babe, eyes scrunched shut
Tiny fists pummelling the air in jerky staccato

Open mouth rooting this way and that
Nuzzling at her mother's warm, milky scented breast.

Earth's Chapel
by Nancy Carlson

Hiking through and around
Pine groves and water.
Birds collecting bits of nourishment
And my favorite,
The sound of the wind at the top of the trees,
Protecting us from the cold.

Such strength, they have
Steadiness, quietness
A big embrace
On this crisp, shadowy day.

Spirits of nature appear as chickadees
Water running quietly under ice
Moving slowly, yet surely
Cushions of pine needles
And crunchy brown leaves
Hills and valleys, ahead and behind.

A visit with Mother Nature, the Earth
Listening to the sounds
Feeling its support
From under my hiking boots
And all around.

'Tis the season of hibernation
Quiet, inward-bound
Grounding, steady and still.

These trees are Lovers
And do what they know is True

So many paths, so many cycles,
Life repeating life.

Noticing the present-ness of this day
Grace…
The fleetingness of everything
Nothing to stop, or make, or do.

Grateful for this expression of life
Reflecting the temporary
And the Eternal One
A living, breathing Chapel of Life.

Orion
by Kai Coggin

I contemplated Orion tonight,
perched high at the midpoint of night,
stretching out his arms and legs into infinity,
one, two, three belted perfection,
Kings in a line.
How is it,
out of all those stars,
in all that seeming chaos and frenzied light,
in all that expanse of untouchable space,
how is it,
that there is that one, two, three
perfect line of light
in the winter's night sky?
The evenly spaced ellipsis written by the hand of God,
an unfinished thought…
a wait, there is more to come…
a star sentence that trails off into silence…

Endless Flight
by Milijana Bozovic

Transparent me
soothing
in You transparent.

Your limpid bosom
and my home,
myself if I am.

Who gave me to You,
Oh, Creative Thought!
And could I live without
You
neutral,
not questioned in existence of maybe nothing.

And could this path
to create our wings for endless flight
be Life without questions?

You and All Things
by Brigid Clare Oak

Do not think Me
distant and cold.
I Am the Warm One
beside you in soft summer grass.
Do not think Me
hard as marble
or breakable as glass.
I Am Breath.
I Am Blood.
I Am Deep Well of Presence.
Find in Me
your cleansing.

Find in Me
your refreshing.
Find in Me
your life, your flow, your peace;
your joy, your song, your sweet release.
Do not think Me
any law but Love;
Love Overshadowing.
Love Enlightening.
Love Encircling.
Love Indwelling.
Love, the Ground
and Growth of All Being.
I Am
The Love,
The Lover,
The Beloved.
I Am the ecstatic
swelling of your soul;
Divinity spilling,
overflowing;
the human heart thrilling,
the human mind knowing.
I Am moist earth's
turning and tilling.
I Am the Hope.
I Am the Healing.
I Am You
and All Things
Made Whole.

11
Voicing Motherhood

"We, like the Mother of the World, become the compassionate presence that can hold, with tenderness, the rising and passing waves of suffering."
Tara Brach

A Symphony of Bird Songs

by Yvonne Brewer

Let us sit in a circle here for a little while where the journey now meets, to honor and give voice to the songs of motherhood. Join me as we unite to listen to the joyful songs, as well as the sad songs that are rarely sung aloud: the ones of loss and struggle.

In the flock of mothers, possibly the first bird many people think about is their own birth mother and their own experiences of being mothered. How wonderful it is to experience the love of one's birth mother, and what a privilege it is, in turn, for that daughter to give birth to a child and see the cycle of motherhood continue in the generations. I am blessed with such an experience.

Within this experience of Motherhood, we celebrate the voices of creation: of birthing new parts of ourselves, as we birth our babies. For the little birds teach us as they grow within us, with us, and through us. Within this nest of nurturing and protecting, motherhood becomes an ongoing continuum that spans generations. For mothers carry past legacies and weave them into new ones, shaping our hearts and connecting us more deeply to the divine universe.

As part of this divine connection, we honor the mothering that goes on all around us, beyond biological motherhood. For many women become mothers without physically giving birth to a baby, but rather, by something that is birthed through a communion with the divine universe or Divine Mother within. We find them within our cultures playing the diverse roles of nurturers and healers, as they feed clients, family, patients, friends and entire communities with Mother Love, bringing us all under their wings. These sensitive souls connect to the very threads of motherhood that are knitted in wombs of Mothers who give birth physically to their creations of life. The selfless, loving nests of these soul-mothers are just as powerful as those of birth mothers.

Motherhood is certainly a path that is filled with diversity, decorated with different colored feathers: some that are accepted by various cultures and some that are not accepted. While motherhood is characteristically filled with love, light and warmth, there are shadows in motherhood that we may sometimes prefer not to acknowledge. There are times when we feel inadequate, unfulfilled or ashamed. We have been labeled as *"Just a Mother"* or *"Only a Single Mother"* or felt bad for being a *"Busy, Working Mother"* or felt we are not enough because we didn't give birth to the children we mother as we are *"Step Mothers"* or *"Adoptive"* or *"Foster"* mothers.

Some mothers are made to feel inadequate because they are in a gay partnership, or because they are transgender mothers, others because they have lost a child in their womb, or were not able to conceive one. There are also those mothers that feel the need to hide their pregnancies, or were forced into a pregnancy, or those who are even pushed to terminate their pregnancies because of other cultural and societal prejudices that dishonor the depth and breadth of motherhood.

The poems that spontaneously emerged for this chapter give voice to many of the aches related to motherhood. As these mothers open their wings and fly through dark clouds, we may hear songs of injustice, loss, discrimination, regret, pain, devastation, shame, neglect, longing and self blame. Yet, woven among them are also tender, joyful, proud melodies that celebrate these mothers' heartfelt commitment to this path: ones that honor their choices, and even the way they navigated their way through a lack of choices.

Let us hold our ears to Mother Earth who carries our very own, singular heartbeat, and listen to every sound that makes a mother: from happy springs bubbling within her, to rumbling earthquakes that split hearts. We embrace *all* Mothers and unite through the same connective thread of divine love that flows through all our hearts. As we read the poems that follow, let us hold a space for the mothers gone before us, heal the generational wounds they have carried, give gratitude for all the mothering love poured on us, offer forgiveness where it may be needed, nurture the mothers of the present, love the divine mother within us, hold our hands out towards the mothers of the future and, above all, celebrate, nourish and remember *who we truly are*, no parts excluded.

Let us bless all Mothers and celebrate the divine feminine energy that has touched our lives in whatever shape or form. May we remember that through each of us flows an individual expression of the divine feminine: We are each a spark of that same flame! Therefore, let us all rise and shine together, even as we give voice to our saddest songs.

We spread our wings together in a circle, harmoniously uniting all the Birds of Motherhood, as our flock holds a singular thread in our beaks, and as we bow to each other and sing: *"We are One Mother"* through all our joys and all our aches as well.

Mothering
by Ruth Calder Murphy

Where there's peace in the place of care,
Mothering's there.
Where there's a soothing of pain,
or human connections that bypass the brain
to strike to the heart of You when the moment's right,
when lonely darkness turns towards the light,
or Divinity winks from Serendipity's face,
when judgment's what you're expecting
and you're given grace…

Mothering comes from old ladies with crinkly smiles
and from little boys who put down their toys a while
to Simply Be, with Me,
from the Spirit of Forests
the ubiquitous Divine,
from the hearts of strangers
who connect with mine…

Sometimes, mothering follows bodily birth
—and sometimes does not,
but flows direct from Mother Earth,
or from the human soul,
bypassing ovaries and wombs and things
and wrapping it, warm, 'round inner children,
nurturing and raising and giving them wings.

Mothering is for everyone, I think, and blesses all.
Mothering is Love and Soul and Heart
—and all with those to share can claim their part.

If I Could
by Maureen Kwiat Meshenberg

If I could scoop up,
a handful of stars—
bouquet of light,
to bring joy to your heart—
I would.
If I could gather up the colors of the rainbow,
cover you with laughter—
bring a smile to your face,
I would.
tender tears that cry now,
life's blows—
have fallen upon you.
I am here child,
but the tears you cry now,
can't be lulled by a lullaby,
once in my arms—
my sweet tender charms,
singing softly in your ear
as I rocked you to sleep.
my heart is broken,
to see your pain—
I want to take it all away,
have you run in a field with children
laughing & playing games.
but sometimes,
in this lost forgotten world-
life can be cruel,
and when you feel like
you have no where to turn,
I am here.
You will find your path,
your creative soul—
of gentleness and spontaneity,
will rise amongst those
who belittle you.

for I will be there,
to cheer you on,
when you feel like you've lost—
when you've actually won.
to see you climb,
high above the rest-
who have scoffed at you,
for you are a diamond
that shines,
illuminating life:
you who are filled with beautiful dreams,
that have yet to come true.

Houses of the Holy
by Jamie Burgess

I have birthed
ecstasy
and
new life
from the darkness
between my hips.
I have nurtured
tiny, beautiful humans
with these bones
housed
within.
They carry my weight,
as well as my burdens,
quietly absorbing
all of my secrets.
They have danced me up
out of the ashes,
supported
my every move,
and breath,
and dream.
Strength

and sinew,
they have proven
their ability to
endure.
They have
whispered
to me
from the moment
of their
creation,
heavily steeped
in magic
and power
and divinity.
God- breathed.

The Child That She Could Not Bring Home
by Yvonne Brewer

They ripped you from my teenage womb,
In a dark loveless room.
They dragged you from my helpless arms, but not from my broken heart.
Stole my child, but didn't steal memories that would tear a soul apart.

The Spring morning that they took you, I sat on a white cold bed,
And I thought,
"I am a Ghost Mother now, walking like the dead,
This bed is like my grave."
And I stared at my little child's future, that I had no power to save.

The Spring morning that they took you,
I was so empty except for a heart filled with sorrows,
Heavy with grief for all the black tomorrows.
So I gave you all I had that day, a heart of sweet golden tears

That I quietly wept as you soundly slept, unaware of your mother's fears.
One tear, for every moment and every year
That I would not be there,
When you cried or when you smiled,
Or wondered did She care?

How I blessed you with my tears of hope and gold,
And begged that somehow your little soul
Would remember the young girl who sat all alone,
That Spring morning,
In that dark loveless room,
Crying, for you,
The child
That
She
Could
Not
Bring
Home.

(This poem was composed in memory of all Mother's who gave birth in "Mother and Baby Homes" in Ireland circa 1920-1970 and in memory of any Mother who was mistreated or forced to put their baby up for adoption.)

Creativity Reborn
by Ulli Stanway

I have closed this painful door
To open a new one
Much more powerful
Than I ever thought possible
I was like a feather
Drifting along
In the longing for a little human soul
To call my own
Tears, so many tears

I have found my place
My silence
Has become my strength
I am content
No child
Not in this lifetime
I am good, so very good
I bless all the mothers out there
For they are god's precious gift
My creative space is mine
My creative flow is ready to be born
I am here
Now
Not lost any longer
In the longings of the future
Stronger, so much stronger than before
My sacred space has lot its silence
The letters like magic dripping from my fingers
My ritual of my own rebirth
In a joyous ceremony
I can feel it coming
My creativity reborn
Everlasting, surprising
From a place of pure joy
And love, so much love
Where love and creativity
Break the chains of self-inflicted suffering
My life
My rebirth.

She Who is Exalted
by Milijana Bozovic

Beauty is She
who surrenders to Life
bringing laughter
to each of our days.

For every fruit
has its precious core:
Give yourself to the muse
that leads you there
and recreate yourself
through her.

As She nourishes
the Primeval Seeds
in every cell of this Timelessness
She gives birth
to Luminous You.

My Angel in the Sky
by Tanielle Childers

The sun outside is shining bright.
Not a cloud up in the sky.
And yet this darkness swallows me whole.
My heart chokes on goodbye.

Sorrow wraps around me tight,
Making it hard to breathe.
And though I know this too shall pass,
For now, I'm asked to grieve.

The life I once held close to mine,
Protected in my womb.
Has died and gone to heaven
And was taken all too soon.

Hold on to those you love so dear.
Memorize the moments as they pass by.
Live, love, laugh all you can
And learn from the tears you're asked to cry.

If nothing ever changed in life,
Butterflies would not be.

And heaven would have no angels,
If God never set them free.

The sun outside is shining bright
Not a cloud up in the sky.
My son's life and death has awakened me.
My heart beats for him this time.

His spirit wraps around me tight
His death so hard to believe.
And yet the light he shines on me,
Gives me all the strength I need.

I miss him so, my beautiful boy
And honor his life by living mine.
I love him still, I always will.
My heart beats for his this time.

Hold on to those you love so dear.
Memorize the moments as they pass by.
Live, love, laugh all you can
And learn from the tears you're asked to cry.

If nothing ever changed in life,
Butterflies would not be.
And heaven would have no angels
If God never set them free.

The sun outside is shining bright.
Not a cloud up in the sky.
If nothing ever changed in life,
Our angels wouldn't fly.

Valentine for a Vacant Womb
by Kai Coggin

This is a Valentine
for what is unborn
in the space
below my belly button.
There is an empty room there,
((my vacant womb))
waiting for divine intervention,
miracles and angels on clouds,
a quiet-filled wanting,
unspoken hoping,
baby, someday maybe,
wish you were now.
I put up curtains
but I won't say what color.
I am building a crib from my ribcage,
and I know that the perfect temperature of milk
will be the warmth that comes out of my breasts.
Baby.
I love you.
Oh god, I love you.
I want to feel you growing into life,
I want to hear your heartbeat rhythm syncopation,
muffled and glowing with mine,
I want to sing to you, silly and sweet,
I want to make up words that you could grow into,
I want to write poems about your smile,
and the light in your eyes,
and how your cry sounds like it might be Heaven,
little one, my little one,
I have cupped my arms into cradle,
and rocked the weight of my spare tire belly to sleep,
and it almost feels like life and giving up, combined.
I did it more than once
even though it made me feel small,
just to practice the moves of mommy,

if you ever come.
This is a Valentine
for how your tiny toes crinkle
when I kiss them for the millionth time,
and how your tiny hand around my finger
makes me feel like I finally belong in this world,
and how you look at me and never look away,
and how you smell like spring rain at any time of day,
and how the sounds you make when dreaming
are enough for me to call music, forever.
Little darling,
I am waiting for you,
here is my open heart,
and my cradle hands,
and somewhere in the stars,
you are wondering where your home will be,
and I am here making myself into a home,
adding windows to my chest,
open-dooring my mouth
so that everything I say is beauty,
and life, and wonder.
I am readying a temple inside
((my vacant womb))
lighting a single candle,
turning poems into lullabies,
painting the ceiling with clouds,
shifting weight on my hips
back and forth
like a constant ocean,
thinking of what name I will call you
that means:
EVERYTHING.

Living Between
by Tracie Nichols

In the space of a breath,
my wild-flashing
crone soul
careens still,
and in slips
the soft mother,
gentle warrior,
fierce child shielder.

A two-sounded whisper,
in a voice familiar,
that's all it takes
to ground
my pestle.
To tame my
furious-beating
heart,
wind-streaming
hair.

In the space of a
breath,
when wild woman
sleep
falls away
broken
by the word
"Mom"
croaked
from the throat
of my suffering
child.

A Child is Born
by Sandra Allagapen

A heart beats
A new world beckons
One loud cry
The child is born
A prayer granted for two
But a blessing for all
Special this babe is
Grace in our lives he brings
For a year or more
No one knows
One thing only is clear
A gift from God he is
A reminder of all that is good
A giver of hope
Look into his eyes and see
The Divine that dwells within
He comes to awaken your heart
Many feelings embracing you
Throughout his life and yours
None as strong as the love
That infuses you
In the end one truth
It matters not how long
A year or more
The blessing remains
He's yours
An eternal bond forged in Heaven
Transcending time and death
Reigniting faith and more
A heart beats
A child is born
Yours or mine
It matters not
Love him we will
For sacred he is.

Rejoice Old Mothers!
by Jennifer Courtney-Zechlin

Rejoice Old Mothers!
Rejoice and wear white.
Delight in your sagging breasts,
once round and full,
now flat against your long chest.
Your babies round and full instead.

Rejoice Old Mothers!
Rejoice and wear green.
Take pride in the ache setting in,
and the wrinkles forming on your hands.
Hands that have tended gardens
and buttoned coats.
Hands that have held the future and rocked her to sleep.

Rejoice Old Mothers!
Rejoice and wear brown.
Admire your aging face.
Eyes still bright, now with drooping lids,
lines turning to crevices all too soon.
Framed by tufts of gray.
This is the face that bravely squared the world
and turned toward the Sun on Summer holidays.
These are the eyes that sparkled brighter than the Christmas lights
and watched as babies were weaned to solid food
and weaned again to Life with solid footing,
Before becoming young mothers—
and fathers—
Someday.

Rejoice Old Mothers!
Rejoice and wear purple.
Wrap yourselves in cloaks of velvet
And crown yourselves with golden gratitude.
For you, Old Mothers, are the queens of this world,

And the heirs to your throne shall someday wear yellow
and hold your legacy in their hearts and homes.
Rejoice Old Mothers! Rejoice!

Emptiness
by Kadambari Kashyap

This emptiness...
For I am just the empty vessel
And you fill me in
With your desire
And there grows a baby
Of the universe,
in the confined infinite
Space of this empty container.
And the plant grows
Out of passion and fire
In receiving our insane desire.
Come, let's embrace each other tight, for here is a prayer:
May this child brought through us rise up, rooted in earth
and bloom out its flowers and fruits to the skies
laughing with the timeless joys of the universe!
Gratitude, gratitude!

The Empty Nest
by Charu Agarwal

You came along
a bright, sunny day
changing my life
in every possible way

My precious bundle—
so helpless and cute
in taking care of you
I was resolute

Could no longer be
footloose, fancy free
I was your lifeline,
you depended on me.

Little by little
you grew on my watch
soon you were giggling
and playing hop-scotch

Having you around
was a source of delight
never mind the occasional
outburst or fight.

Our time together
I took for granted then
not knowing you'd take off,
at a tender ten!

"Mom I'll do it,
even though I'm afraid"
you said to me,
in a voice so sedate.

My heart filled with joy,
gratitude and pride
but later that night,
grief-struck, I cried.

I knew all along
it was the right thing to do
I had to let go,
how? I hadn't a clue.

The preparations started,
the months were few
then all too soon,

it was time for adieu.

The axe fell between us,
separating me from you
I thought my heart
would break into two

With anguish and pain
running deep in my chest,
I came home without you,
to an empty nest.

12
Voicing Love

"Don't forget love;
it will bring all the madness you need
to unfurl yourself
across the universe."
Mirabai

And There is Love...
by Nancy Carlson

So much poetry is written about love. Love poems are in all cultures, from ancient texts and songs to the present day. They are woven into prayers, music and song, published in books and in the hearts of many. Poetry, in general, is an art form, which has the qualities of beauty, grace and intense emotions. How perfect a way to describe love! In its written words, it expresses that which has no words, and is searching for meaning. It is a place to speak our truths and connect to feeling, sometimes a paradox: ethereal and otherworldly.

Love can be heart breaking, and heart filling. It can be simple, sweet and pure or grand in its expansion...with a bigness that feels endless and everywhere. At times, we keep our love tucked-in and close to our hearts. Other times, we let our heart open to others. Love expresses itself with an ebb and flow, as all of nature does. Its essence exists in all of nature and everyone. It is known to be timeless, within all space and is an energy that lasts forever.

There are endless expressions of love with its many qualities, forms and perceptions of what love is. Truly, love is multifaceted! Have you heard that love has no rules, no boundaries, is universal, unconditional, selfless and connected to us all? It is deep, real, a feeling, spoken, unspoken and more than just a thought. There are endless possibilities with love! Love is ageless, not controlling, passionate, beautiful, heartache, mystic and at its best, exists in every present moment.

Love can break us apart and put us back together. Love is always present, waiting for the door to our hearts to open to its presence. Even in the in the dark places, love is there when we can't see it. Longing, grieving, loss and self-abandonment are in the flow of love. Romantic love can have conditions, expectations, come with complications and truly be a form or reflection of love, in another way.

But love, in its deepest self, has no conditions. In its true intimacy, there is trust, surrender and opening to a higher form of guidance.

It speaks… "I will always love you, all of you". Love is our birthright. Fear is its obstacle. Love is a choice and a way of being. We bring love with us into our life as a gift to ourselves, and for all others who interact with us. I ask you: "How can we make more room for this love to be expressed in our lives? How much love can our dear hearts hold? How can we share our love, be love and surrender to love all at the same time?" Some say that love is "heaven on earth". Perhaps that is because all is possible when there is love, all is healed, and all is Love.

These following poems represent a small part of this…." Love is a many splendored thing…".

The Search
by Darshana Mahtani

This heart is a cage for my love,
It does not fit.
This body with all my organs
In chambers
Is like a submarine
Sinking me
From my being.
All of these things you can touch
And feel
They are not enough.
If you think you're in love,
Dig deep.
If you think you're being loved,
Dig deeper.
If you think you love yourself,
Dig honey.
There is a place
Where love is more
Than a thought,
Or a feeling or a verb,
Love is an energy
That flows from the rivers
To the seas to the trees
Over hills and into
You and me.

Heart Hugs
by Krista Katrovas

Let us, "Undress the World,"
Untie the knots
Wrapped around our hearts.
Let's loosen those ties, extend
A warm glance, a friendly smile,
And even if we don't seem

In need of one,
Let's reach out and hug others.
Let's press our hearts to theirs,
Overlap them, hearts talk in this way,
They console, listen, and live as one,
'Cause heart hugs
Are kin to fire,
And too can burn away
That which we no longer need.
And when we embrace one another,
Let's inhale deeply,
Take in what needs to be healed,
Exhale what needs to be freed.
Through our breathing in unison
Let's place that which no longer serves our
Highest Selves
Into universal love
Where all and everything that enters
Dances into fullness.
Then whisper into their ear,
As you consciously press your heart to theirs,
"Hearts know how to hear,
They hear, even when our heads
Forget to listen."
Let's bring our mind and heart
Closer to one another,
Create less distance between them.
And when we hold one another
In this way,
We know we are in the midst
of heaven.

Stone
by Shailie Dubois

I held a small stone and a wave came over me
Washing the sediment of falseness
I spoke to the stone and heard an echo

Embellishing the heart with truthfulness
I brought the stone to my lips and tasted
The fullness of life in its sweetness
I sat with the stone in silence
It spoke, 'Made with love by love.'

She Thanks the Universe for Loving Her
by Laura Demelza Bozma

I love my friend for using her voice
how easy can life be?
I just love her for that!
For ages we could live
inside of a shell
curled up like yin and yang.

She doesn't need to do anything
I just follow what I call
'The Geisha's red fragrance'
that's where she
slowly moves between the books
she sleeps inside of them
with this stories to swim in.

Sometimes I stand besides her
as she sleeps to wave away
the kingfishers in awe
with the letters I write her
my dilemma is
I love their color in her dreams
but don't want them to wake her up.

I see her doing everything
I just love her for that!
How easy can life be?
watching a little robin
hopping from leaf to leaf
how faithful is she

kissing my soul
with the red of a Robin's chest
every time she flies into my stillness.

If there is only this one Island
we should live in it
for here is the spark:
the medicine for the dying breed
the poems
in which we should build our home.

I've got lungs with enough air
to love her as long as my heart beats
through her I am love
through her I learn everything
about flying up
and finding a star
in the thick blanket of night

Everything is all right
my universe
I love you.

We are Love
by Carolyn Riker

All that is love is not always spoken,
It is felt by the trees, sea, wind and earth.

Love is a tempest and when broken,
the shattered discourse will quiver a rebirth.

Heartache will ignite a mystical mend,
from the darkest scripts, folded, shattered and torn.

We grasp at the depths of our spirit and bend,
rising stronger and clearer, no longer forlorn.

Letting go of the illusions, we embrace a galaxy,
a nebulous of intense creative love.

Seeing our existence as stardust, isn't a fallacy,
to be loved, to feel love is infinite as a rising dove.

Love is All There Is
by Ulli Stanway

Love knows no borders
Time fades in its presence
Love is without age
It knows no black, nor white
No you or me
It has a language of its own
It feels the space between our souls
True love does not wish control
It chooses the gentle flow of endless possibilities

Love allows growth
And undermines all we are
It breaks us into pieces
And sometimes we stop to breathe
Love is the agony of unfilled desires
Whilst dancing in a passionate first embrace

Sometimes love wears off
It gets so very tired of the ups and downs
That it leaves for a while
Or maybe forever
To be rediscovered
On a new day
With a different soul's beating heart
Love in all its ever-changing beauty
She moves in mysterious ways

The day sad eyes catch a glimpse of it
Unkissed lips finally meet their fortune

For the first time
When reality is more beautiful than the story
The best of all dreams did ever tell
That day love history was made
Another piece in the mosaic of her endless ways

You shall not anchor love in another's soul
For it wants to be washed ashore gently
Without the use of force
Love asks you to allow it into your own heart
You must not ever doubt love itself
It is the ever-present force of life
A shadow of death
It is all around
It lights up the darkest corners
And switches off our lights
Whilst creating timeless space

Some say love is a choice
Some say he who loves is a fool
Others claim that there is no love

For me love is all there is
My heart is wide open
I allow love to be omnipresent
With every breath I take
I immerse myself in its gifts
Love is all there is
Love is all there ever will be!

Back In Our Hearts
by Krista Katrovas

She sat looking out the window
at leaves moving effortlessly to wind.
She observed nature,
in the quiet of Sundays,
one of the few days of the week

she was free to do, be, as she need only be,
or so she thought.

The leaves at times
seemed comfortably still
only to move again to the breath of wind.
As if the wind itself were a choreographer
showing each leaf how to bend in air.
They'd flip over sometimes
then softly fall to the ground
like a baby lulled in a cradle.
She wanted to live more like these leaves,
like a baby resting without worry,
without sound,
with only breath to guide her.

"Love is what we are born with. Fear is what we learn,"
Marianne Williamson said.
And with this life spent with "unlearning,"
she sat watching the leaves,
learning new ways to be,
how to move through the week,
in a soft, breath-like fashion,
reserved beyond Sunday mornings,
and recalled the days she resided in her heart.
She hugged the child, and the adult self within, and said,
"I love the front, sides, and also,
the back of your heart."

Opening To Love
by Elizabeth Muccigrosso

I love the space between your words
Suspended time
drenched in blue stars
electrically ignited
deep knowing
hidden in pockets of ecstasy.

I love the waves that vibrate behind your voice
when you quietly say
" I love you,"
pulling my ear in closer.

The spring ushers the phase of light
beneath which, rivers begin to flow,
warms the ice,
trickles between crevices
down the long steep run.

I have waited.

Long have I watched for the rush,
sought it in dammed up pools.
Unable to move
stopped by walls.

It wasn't until I walked beside your stream
that I heard you,
felt your mist caress me.

I stepped into the flow
and in a cascade of timelessness
your resonance shivered my roots.

Soaked in your love
I now stand,
a tender shoot
beautifully forming
wrapped in my softened husk
ecstatically awaiting for you to peel me open.

And We Would Be Free
by Zoe Quiney

I'd like you to understand me,
The way the moon understands
The ocean.
To trace your hands along my soul
Like waves as they gently kiss
The shore.

I'd like you to take my hand
And hold a thousand different lives;
Reincarnated wishes and desires
Nestled against your skin.

You would paint my dreams
Among the stars,
Taking me to other worlds
With your words.

Our hearts would find the answers
To every forgotten question;
As we strip away the layers
To reveal our souls.

And we would be free.

If I Leave
by Alice Maldonado Gallardo

Do not worry if I leave.
Do not cry and suffer.
I only left one dream,
you will find me in another.

I will embrace you in stardust
while you sleep.
I will enter your heart,

I will become part of you,
and guard it forever.
My light in every cell,
in every breath,
in every beat
of your soul.

My strength is now your strength.
Take from me what you need.
I will be the dragonfly
teaching you how to live.

If I leave,
just smile,
close your eyes,
and find me inside
the womb of eternity.

If I leave,
just remember the light in my eyes
when I looked at you.
Nourish your soul
with my love
being reborn in you,
that is how you heal a wound.

If I leave,
promise me
that you will let me free
from all anguish and guilt.
Do not capture me
in your pain.
Do not hold me
inside your fears.

Let me free to roam
the beginning and the end
of the universe.

Let me free to fire
each and every star.

If I leave,
let me be
free.

Enlightenment Catalyst
by Jai Maa

Enlightenment Catalyst,
Carry on beyond this world of delusion and sentiment.
The imprint of safety and love mastery you left traveling in the winds of your every breath enlightened kings and queens who were fortunate to walk this planet the same time you did, Earth Angel.
You said this was the last time you would incarnate here.
And that was made undoubtedly clear by the effortless grace you gave to every ignoramus who projected self-hatred in your face.
I watched you stand there,
time and time again,
turning the cheek, Mary Madeline, you have shined your Christ-Light in this Day of the Goddess.
Without retaliation.
Without harm.
Without sin.
Instead, you prayed for them.
Gave to them, generously.
Without glory.
There are very few who are fortunate to know you like I do.
You took birth in a world not yet worthy of your fame.
You played life consciously and detached like video game.
Not concerning yourself with the mundane surface appearance.
You were alchemizing Hell's program through meditation to give our entire world clearance into a Heaven on Earth we might never feel grateful for.
Many of us ignore the simplicity of beauty you realized in your short life.

What is it like?
To look through your Christ eyes?
Mary Madeline,
Enlightenment Catalyst,
Earth Angel.
I watched you love fearlessly.
I watched you wish mercy for those who wished you harm.
I watched you, delicate and unarmed purify the world's hatred in
   your very own heart.
I watched cancer eat your body like acid eroding the chains that
   kept your pure soul captive to a world unworthy of you.
You knew your angelic presence and mere breath was something
   your life could never repay.
Still you chose to take birth here anyway.
You chose to create,
against the sands of time,
lessened by lessons you learned too quickly, Earth Angel,
Heaven on Earth is restored by you simply taking birth.
You continue to enlighten our world with your breath,
still traveling in the winds,
leaving imprints
of safety and love mastery.

In loving memory of Mary Madeline Day

The Dance of Life and Love
by Savitri Talahatu

Dance when Life flows through you
Dance when the Holy Name takes over you
Dance when there is no more you or me
Dance and let Love express Itself through you
Dance when Life and Love merge within you
Dance and live Life freely and ecstatically
Dance and send Love wherever It wants to go
Dance in gratitude of the possibility.

Shared Love
by Jennieke Janaki

Love that Is
Shared
Forever
Heart opening
A precious lasting joyful moment
Our innate connection
Deeply felt
Blissful Existing
We remember
It flowers unconditionally
Beyond reasonable logic
Connected
Blessed and grateful
An opportunity to lose our little self
Open for Spiritual Realization
Though Vulnerable
Lost
Painful when gone
Left with an empty feeling
I Know, I Feel
You forever with me
Shared Love
Together as One
The Divine bandage
Our Medicine
In Foreverness
Never alone
Cradled in the arms of sacred Love
Protected
Safe
At Home
In Immortal Peace.

13
Voicing Our Sisterhood

"A sister is a gift to the heart, a friend to the spirit,
a golden thread to the meaning of life."
Isadora James

United by the Pages of Our Journey
by Maureen Kwiat Meshenberg

We are the women, who have gathered with words spoken in the circle of our breath: the voices of our poetry, echoing through the pages of our journey. We have held ourselves open to vulnerability, allowing it to become our courage. We have faced the fiery breath of fear, only to embrace our true power. We have dried the tears that stained our hearts with words like ointment on our bruised souls.

With these words that come from our hearts to the page, we have released our voices together in sisterhood. We write with words that can break the silence or bring us to our quiet pause. "I write this poem as a hand reaching out to the broken, I plant my words next to their abandoned seeds." *Kai Coggin*. Our voices can be strong, purposeful and powerful. Our voices can reveal our imperfections, and how we move through them with lessons that draw us toward compassion and grace. "And you are allowed to make all the mistakes you need in order to best carve out your niche." *Alise Versalla*

More than friend, I call you sister. The power that is created in the bond of sisterhood is like no other. I have seen women rise through the corridors of time with fearless tenacity and quiet thunder. Crossing bridges that crumble behind them, but hand in hand they find their strength in stepping forward together. I have seen women rush to each other's side when life has broken us wide open. Our blood, are the tears that become our ocean within. Our laughter brings us to a joy that makes us soar in the sky of our souls.

The poems that grace this chapter speak of this sweet bond between women. Often created out of devastation, these poignant poems also reveal an honoring that transcends cultures, races and religions. For when we reach our place of gathering, where our voices are united, we blend into a single hum: the hum of our souls. "There's power in connections, in the meeting of minds, in serendipity and synthesis across dividing lines." *Ruth Calder Murphy*

These poems speak of the circling of friendship: our universal connection to each other. When we speak in the language of our poetry, we bravely enter into another soul sister's heart, leaving our words as a delicate imprint. "Bravery replacing trepidation one breath at a time, grace discovered at the bottom of the exhale." *Anita Grace Brown*

Our poems can bring comfort, laughter, and mindfulness; we bring with us words of imagination, allegorizing our birthing, our dying, and our transitioning, again and again. We hold these words in every part of our body, in our movement, in our dancing with the beating of our very own hearts. "Hips that have been the keepers of hidden temples, hips with a timeless, unspeakable wisdom that has birthed history and will birth the future." *Dominique Youkhehpaz*

"She loves me I love her and this will always be." *Shailie Dubois*. When coming from this place of love, it is "love" that loves through us. It surpasses human love with its limitations, we open up to bringing ourselves to a compassionate and grace-filled love. Some of our friendships only touch in passing just as a glimpse or a brushing of fingertips. Some friendships hold our lives for years, as we embrace each other for our entire lives. "It is impossible to compress the decades into verse and a river of memories into words…" *Ginny Brannan*. We enter the circle of our belonging, whether it is for a season, or for a lifetime. Our stories hold us close to each other, as we see them overlap our lives and our living. "We formed a circle, sent whirls of dreams, heart visions, shared our heart wrenching life stories." *Krista Katrovas*

Our sisterhood holds us in our own universe; we move with each other to a special rhythm and hold our truths in the galaxy of our shining. "Our words like stars that scatter across the universe of our lives. We do not die but bring glimmer just like those who have shined before us." *Maureen Kwiat Meshenberg*

We come to releasing of our words to the world for all to read and hold close to their hearts. So dear ones who read these pages: "Embrace your desire, hug your fire!" *Marine L. Rot*. Come and enter into the Universe of words like stars that glisten upon your journey as we share with you *our* journey. "These things are not for naught, for you dear one are an integral part, the dust of stars, a glistening heart, a soul on fire, a work of sacred art." *Carol Reedy Rogero*

"My Star Sister, allow me to thank you for teaching me how to shine in both the dark and the light." *Krista Angelique Katrovas.* Our dearest and selfless Star Sister, Catherine Ghosh, has opened this universe for us through the Journey of the Heart, Women's Spiritual Poetry Project. She has opened a gateway for us to share our voices and enter into them in a timeless space of belonging. So in this final chapter, where we write our voices onto the pages of our journey, we express our honoring to Catherine, and all other Star Sisters in the world like her. We express our honoring to each other because such Star Sisters open the space for us to awaken the Star Sister in ourselves. We are ever so grateful for the allowing of our words to grace these pages. "I honor you, dear woman, inspiration that touches my soul. I bow to you, with clasped hands holding your heart close to mine." *Maureen Kwiat Meshenberg*

There Have Always Been Women's Hips
by Dominique Youkhehpaz

Through centuries of sunrises and sunsets,
There have always been women's hips.

Hips swaying under the stars,
dancing to the rhythm of the wind,
singing the songs of our ancestors,
worshiping the very life they create.

Before man discovered fire and electricity,
There have always been women's hips.

Hips beaming with fire and light,
exuding aliveness.
Source of renewable energy,
The reason for evolution
and incentive for revolutions,
The birthplace of desire,
Hips blossoming, seducing, inviting, receiving.
Wild, innocent hips.

Waves of change ripple across the planet
Like earthquakes,
Every time a woman shakes her hips.

Before the invention of the telescope or Einstein's theory of
    relativity,
There have always been women's hips.

Hips navigating new territories and opening to unknown places,
Hips throbbing with creativity,
Hips that invented inventors.
Hips that ruled countries,
And hips that ruled the rulers of countries.

Hips held captive by ideas
And hips that could not be contained.
hips that carried us home.

Before there was tantra,
Before there was pornography and prostitution,
There have always been women's hips.

Hips giving birth to the senses,
To eyes, ears, mouths, noses, and lips.
Hips intimate with pain and writhing with pleasure.

Hips that gave everything,
And hips that held back,

Shamed hips, numb hips,
Hips revered and respected,
Abused and exploited,
hurt, healed, loved and feared,

Hips that have tasted tongues
And hips that have tasted razor blades,

Hips frozen in fear,
Hips afraid to open,
And hips fully awakened to their power.

Through world wars and cold wars,
Through genocide and suicide,
Through poverty and famine,
There have always been women's hips.

The beginning of sorrow,
The first spark of hope.

Hips shedding blood and tears
In rhythm with the moon,
Mourning the monthly death of potential life,

Guiding us into the darkness.

Hips birthing saints and murderers,
Lovers and fighters,
Hafiz and Hitler.

Hips birthing hungry children,
Hips birthing slaves and their oppressors.
Hips birthing freedom.

Hips trembling with the pulse of life.

Before there was geography,
Before there was science,
There have always been women's hips.

Hips of every spice and every flavor:

Rose hips,
Soft hips,
Bony hips,
Clumsy hips.

Arab hips,
African hips,
Palestinian and Israeli hips,
Jewish and Christian hips,
Atheist hips,
Faithful hips, promiscuous hips,
Brokenhearted hips.

Silent hips,
Silenced hips,
And hips with French accents.

Universal, unconditional hips.

Through the endless cycle of
Birth, old age, sickness, and death,
There have always been women's hips.

Hips that have been the keepers of hidden temples.

Hips with a timeless, unspeakable wisdom,
that has birthed history
And will birth the future.

Hips within hips within hips
Darkness within darkness
The gateway to all understanding.

Hips pregnant with possibilities
And intimate with the truth.

Hips that have passed down the secret of the universe
in a language
Hidden in hieroglyphics of sensation,
decoded every time a woman
Inhabits her hips.

We Who Have Gathered
by Maureen Kwiat Meshenberg

we who have gathered,
with our words—
our stories,
our breath—
letting them rise,
into the full moon sky.
our souls that hold,
our words like stars—
that scatter,
across the universe
of our lives,
we do not die—

but bring glimmer.
just like those who
have shined before us.
we sisters,
who hold the moon,
so close to the—
beating of our hearts,
the shifts she brings
tethers us together,
as we sing our stories—
on the pages of our journey.
super moon,
we encircle you
with our truths,
our trials,
our tears that—
fall upon our dancing:
gently ever laughing,
as we sing our words,
to the sky that holds
the women's moon so high,
on this August night.

A Message to My Sisters
by Alise Versella

Remember you are beautifully
Imperfectly human
The very act of your being here straight from the cosmos is in fact a miracle
One I'm sure aliens in other Milky Way galaxies are sitting up on their hovercrafts Attempting to figure out
You can bleed
You can cry
You can feel
The warm touch of my hand
You can laugh
You can smile

And you're allowed to get mad
But don't hold a grudge; it's bad for the heart
Growing up is hard
You live in a rough and tumble world
It spins, I think, for the sole purpose to get you dizzy just so it can see itself knock you down
But remember how miraculously it was you got here and stand back up
Dust your vibrant, bloody knees
And wipe away the salt- the same salt from the sea
How miraculously it can come from your eyes when you cry and wash away the pain
Like antiseptic in a cut
Don't forget that words are just letters strung together and that even though they can sting they can create beautiful phrases when they fall from the right lips
Remember that you have limbs you need only to keep limber and strong
Take care of your body because it holds your soul,
Your heart
The essence of your being
The star dust you still have inside your veins
And give thanks to that temple everyday
Remember that you are a strong
Wise
Mysterious
Seductive
Woman
And men will never fully comprehend your powers
And other women are not so in tune to their cosmic witchy ways and they will only be Jealous of the fact that you figured it out for yourself so much sooner than they did
Give yourself a chance to grow
Because even the dandelion weed
In the corner of the yard
Will bloom golden if left to do so
Let the world in all its burning fires be your not-so-favorite teacher
Listen to the ways she tells you to line your eyes

And coat your lashes
And paint your pouting lips
And walk in those stilettos to elongate your legs
And how to dress to show off the best parts of your body
Because you are still a pretty girl who wants to be a beautiful
    woman
Let her teach you the wonders she has to offer a young girl
But don't let her dictate your world
You are the ruler of your niche on this planet
And you are allowed to make all the mistakes you need in order to
    best carve out your niche
But listen when I tell you how to walk away and avoid the
    mistakes I've already made
The ones I know others made
The ones I know will really, truly hurt you
Listen first and trust your gut
It will steer you true
When you heart is blind
And your brain is tired
Cultivate passions and be content with those passions satisfying
    your soul instead of your Bank account
Let your skies turn gray sometimes as well
Because the moonlight shines brightest in the darkest nights
And when you find yourself lost—which you might from time to
    time
Look deep into your irises
You'll see a piece of cosmos still glinting there
The starlight lingering
To remind you from whence you came.

I Honor You
by Maureen Kwiat Meshenberg

I honor you,
dear woman—
inspiration that,
touches my soul.
I bow to you,

with clasped hands
holding your heart,
close to mine.
We gather in sunsets,
by full moons,
in the seasons turning,
and we drum,
to the beating feet
of our dancing.
My offering,
I now bring—
I honor you:
your beauty,
your soul,
your heart,
your tears,
that spill
upon my face.
Our laughter,
that sings
when we hold,
our circling—
around the day,
of our coming.
In the time of,
my awakening
you held me,
in the sacred space—
in the time of my breaking,
you wrapped me
in your arms.
I reflect you,
you reflect me,
pass our failures—
we bring victory,
in brilliance,
we shine in each-
other's shadow,
with our infinite light.

Sister
by Marine L. Rot

Sister,

Let go of pride,
But remember, you're not here to hide.

Smallness is cute,
But magnificence is your size.

For you cannot pretend...

Those who made you descend,
were just a mind chatter.

Embrace your desire.
Hug your fire!

Come closer, get it now,

Sister.

Old Friends
by Ginny Brannan

As each one speaks,
I watch the years fall away
through eyes that remember
            the girls we once were—

Together again...
we pick up where we left off
never missing a beat,
            ever moving forward.

It is impossible to compress

the decades into verse
and a river of memories
                into words…

Their friendships sustain me—
each one a treasured pulse
        inside this grateful heart.

Golden Bauble
by Anita Grace Brown

set right in the center of her wildly beating
heart
real or imagined
the gem lies cushioned
amid
layers upon layers
of bubble wrap
and fancy gauze
hidden deeply enough
safe from harm

exquisite in its perfectly
bewitching and well-formed
luminosity

she prizes its strength
spun from tenacity
and gilded passions on

one occasion she steps
toward uncharted
treasures
in a future
stripped away of defenses

bravery replacing
trepidation one breath at a time

grace discovered at the bottom of the
exhale

a rare glimpse of the precious stone
Hmmmm… a bit tarnished
chipped on one side
you love it all the more!
for it
was **never** unmarred
or fragile

it's worth
derived
not from artistry
or symmetry
but
from the artist
herself
who fashioned it.

Women's Tipi Time
by Krista Katrovas

We sat close to the fire,
poking it, adding wood,
watching the smoke
rise before escaping
through the funnel
of the tipi.
We formed a circle,
sent whirls of
dreams,
heart visions,
shared our heart wrenching life stories
mostly that men had burnt into our lives,
and placed them into the hands
of our ancestors
for them to carry.

Those prayers
are surely to find their way
into the trees
during this season of change
among the rusty leaves
that now break and fall
then land on the animal hide floor.

We, ladies, slept.
Head to the fire,
tossing in the night,
switching sides
when our child bearing hipbones
grew sore
from the hardening, cold ground.

Late in the night,
I took T.P. from the grocery bag
hanging in the tipi,
squatted outside,
spotted a shooting star between the canopy of trees.
From those woods
who take women's burdens away.
I wished peace
for whatever may come of us all.

Connections
by Ruth Calder Murphy

There's power in connections
—in the meetings of minds,
the touching of fingertips,
the sparks that fly
as live wires converge
and the consummate union
of elements.
There's power in the frisson

of pennies dropping—
in the moment when night
turns to day
and darkness slides away
on the bare back of Dawn.
There's power in connections
— in you
and I—
in our word-thoughts
and shape-thoughts,
in melody
and harmony
and the idiosyncrasies
of our individual beats.
There's power
in our voices,
in the movement of our bodies,
in our colors painted boldly,
in our dancing feet…
There's power in connections
— in the meeting of minds—
in serendipity
and synthesis
across dividing lines.

Star Sister
by Krista Angelique Katrovas

Though we are not sisters
by blood,
we are sisters of life,
which often runs deeper
than shared DNA.

You are my Star Sister.
You shine brightly
as you serve your elders,
when others choose to walk away.

You bring joy to their final days,
and ride the waves of emotions
that the end of life brings,
like those Floridian waters
on your long board that you surf,
"Surfer girl, Surfer girl."

We laughed at your getting stung
by a jellyfish
in your eye
because of how humorous
you made it all sound.
You focused on the rarity
of such a thing happening
rather than on the pain of it.
You are my Star Sister
as you so often
choose to shine brightly.

You taught me,
continue to teach me,
that we, like stars,
are, too, in need of darkness,
in order to see our brightest.

You remind me of the dark,
how its opposite, the light,
will return,
and how darkness is a blessing,
reminding us
and teaching us
of the light found
on shiny days,
and that this is why
we need the dark days, too.

You are my Star Sister
and you shine

"Like the Moon, and the Stars and the Sun,"
you remind me
like the Beatles sung,
that "We all shine on,"
and so today,
on this dark night of your soul,
allow me to remind you,
you are a star,
keep shining,
my Star Sister,
allow me to *thank you*
for teaching me,
how to shine
in both the dark
and the light.
I stand in return
as your Star Sister
shining brightly
when your light is too dim
for you to see.

Abandoned Seeds
by Kai Coggin

On the westernmost tip of Africa,
in the republic of Senegal,
there is a village surrounded
by ocean and desert and forest,
a land of contradictions and secrets,
of ritual and initiation,
a terrain of beaten spirits,
where women walk in circles
with clipped wings and dragging feet,
broken before blooming,
dust storms rising
up to an unforgiving sky,
holding questions like, "what did I do to deserve this?"
and, "somebody please tell me, why?"

The full moon hesitantly rises
knowing it is the impetus for barbarism,
knowing that when it reaches high in the African night,
there will be a different kind of howling.
The women of the tribe gather
their daughters, from babies to teenagers,
and walk across the empty desert,
across the Gambia river
and into the Casamance region
where there is a lush, green canopy of trees
that can muffle the sounds
of ritual tyranny
being passed down like a gift.
They reach the sacred forest,
the soil is rich with blackness,
almost purple it's so black,
blood-dirt mixture of earth,
where the clitoris
of a 7 year old girl,
is
cut
off
and left buried
in the ground
like an abandoned seed,
and then another's seed… seed… seed… seed…
until the forest floor becomes a garden of loss.
Her budding seed is stolen in the night,
by the hands of her own tribeswomen,
in the name of ritual,
in the name of initiation,
in the name of tradition
religion, superstition, womanhood, ignorance and fear,
and because her mother's mother
littered this same forest with skin and screaming.
Millions of seeds severed and scattered over time,
disembodied with dull blades by guilty, guilty hands.
On this night, maybe three dozen girls are cut,

mothers pushing young backs to unforgiving dirt,
legs held open, under a moon that cannot close its eyes.
I can only imagine the color that the soil becomes
when mixed with that much blood,
the hollow scream of a clitoris falling in the forest,
where other women pretend not to hear the sound… of grief.
The young girl is sewn closed,
leaving only two holes,
sewn closed as tribal songs and incantations
lull her into a state of surrender.
Her legs are tied together to keep her from moving,
and she must lay there on her back
underneath the moon for two weeks,
while her emptiness becomes a painful scar,
a sacred ground of betrayal,
a question never asked or answered.
A tribesman will not marry an uncut woman.
An uncut woman is seen as a whore,
an insatiable sex-monger,
unwanted and unclean.
She will not be worth the ox and sheep
that her father will accept as dowry.
She will be shunned in the village
and live a life of solitude and desperation.
For hundreds of years,
spanning countless countries and tribes
this practice has carried on,
passed down as ceremonial certainty
from mothers to daughters,
as natural and necessary to life
as learning to walk, or fetching the water, or skinning a goat.
In 2012, the United Nations General Assembly
passed a worldwide resolution
to ban all forms of Female Genital Mutilation,
classifying it as a human rights violation and child abuse,
and hopefully the woman of Senegal, Africa
have heard the declaration,
have put down their dulled blades,

and let the full moon rise
without the need to plant anymore tender stolen seeds.
This is not a geography lesson, though,
that is to say, there are millions of women living all over the world
that have been robbed of the mountaintop of their sexual pleasure.
There are thousands of girls that still do not understand
what was taken from them and why.
Senegal is not the only land that cuts off unripe fruit.
I write this poem
as a hand reaching out to the broken,
I plant my words
next to their abandoned seeds,
next to the holy spring buds
blooming on the floor of the sacred forest
that took something so sacred to them.
I stand under the lush canopy
and listen for the signs of healing,
a cool breeze,
a river joining the ocean,
a bird's distant song.
I visualize an invisible wall around the forest,
where no one with a dull blade
or backward cultural intentions may enter.
I stand in the light of my words,
to free what is buried in the darkness,
to sing a song for the women that have survived,
as they live their lives, as they birth their babies,
as they flourish into who they have the strength to become.
I light a circle of fire underneath a full moon,
and see them all with phoenix wings,
rising from the ashes of broken,
into
Goddess.

The Dance That Bears Your Name
by Carol Reedy Rogero

This is for the "misfits",
the odd ones,
the seekers of light,
the unveilers of darkness,
the back row learners,
the silent observers,
the artists hidden within,
the blenders-in
and the standers-out,
the ones with faraway eyes
and the ones that pierce,
the ones with velvet tongues
and those with truth-telling lips,
the ones who seek
and the ones who find,
the ones who dream
and the ones that rhyme,
the ones who pour themselves all in
and hold their breath,
the ones who lay it on the line
and take a stand.
These things you are,
are not for naught,
for you dear one
are an integral part,
the dust of stars,
a glistening heart,
a soul on fire,
a work of sacred art.
Fan the flames
of your intrepid soul
and dance the dance
that bears your name.

She and I
by Shailie Dubois

We teeter and totter
Dipping our toes into pain and into joy
Oftentimes diving
Never without laughter in our pockets
And well equipped with song
Between it all we rest
Our hearts bound with a sacred truth
She loves me
I love her
And this will always be.

"One woman is a tiny divine spark in a timeless sisterhood tapestry collective; All of us are Wild Women."
Jan Porter

About the Authors

Charu Agarwal is a yoga teacher, holistic therapist and writer who is passionate about helping people connect to the wisdom, love and peace residing deep inside our hearts. She loves to read, contemplate, commune with nature, travel and share the joy of living with her husband and daughter. Visit charuagarwal-yoga.com for more.

Vrinda Aguilera is a Montessori trained primary school teacher, an intuitive energy healer, a poet, and practitioner of Bhakti yoga. She is passionate about supporting women on their spiritual journey. She lives in rural Florida with her husband and three children where she blossoms in the experience of being a mother.

Zahra Akbarzadeh is an Iranian mother, cardiologist, fellowship in echocardiography, author of the published article: *Cosmic Music; Insight into the Theory of Love*, a certified teacher of Integral Deep Listening-Dream-yoga, who translated the book, "Ending Nightmares for Good," into Persian, and co-author with Jon Frederickson of the forthcoming book "Humility."

Sandra Allagapen is originally from Mauritius but now lives in London where accountancy, healing therapies, jewelry making and poetry are some of the colors on the palette of her life. She dreams of spending more time in Italy one day and loves books, crystals and long summer evenings. Contact Sandra at www.empoweredheart.co.uk

Helene Averous is a mother who has found peace in the depth of the heart after an intense self-inquiry. Her journey transformed her from an active executive woman to the author of picture books for kids about colors and a mystic/Zen poetry book, "Silent Drops". More info on www.heleneaverous.com.

Heather Awad has been writing poetry for about ten years. She never sought publishing while she was raising her daughter, or returning to school to finish her Bachelor's Degree. She plans to work in the field of probation once she graduates. Heather believes that some things come and go, but poetry is here to stay.

Laura Demelza Bosma (1986) is a Dutch singing and painting poetess an doula living in Austria where she gave birth to two lovely children. She follows the river of life and loves to spend time caring for her roots, just by beingwhere she is, wherever she may be. Mothergoddesspoetry.blogspot.com

Milijana Bozovic lives in Montenegro, Southeastern Europe. She is 24 years old and she works as a translator for English, Russian and Montenegrin languages. She writes from her childhood, mainly poetry. She is interested in art as life and freedom for all.

Ginny Brannan resides in Massachusetts with her husband, son and two cats. Starting her poetic journey in 2009, her poetry has been included in *The dVerse Anthology: Voices of Contemporary World Poetry*, and *Journey of the Heart: An Anthology of Spiritual Poetry by Women*. Follow her at: insideoutpoetry.blogspot.com

Yvonne Brewer lives in Cork, Ireland where she has been a teacher, community worker, reiki master, wife, poet, etc. But it is only since Yvonne heard the words *"Mum"* that she felt fully alive and living her true life's purpose, as motherhood has bought her many gifts such as self-awareness and blossoming creativity.

Anita Grace Brown lives in NJ with her husband, two teenagers and golden retriever. They live by the family mantra, "Either everything is a MIRACLE or nothing is!". She enjoys keeping life simple and full of natural beauty, writing as spiritual practice, yoga, cooking and meditation. Anita Grace enjoys sharing her gifts at SmilingheartYoga.org.

Jamie Burgess is a wild, creative, adventurous heart. She is a mama, writer, doula, photographer, tree-hugger, stargazer, avid reader and music lover. Her heart's desire is to encourage and inspire others with her art and life. She is committed to living with courage, daily, and following her heart, always.

Kim Buskala considers herself a free spirit: she flies by the seat of her pants. Kim feeds her soul by embracing family, nature and the arts. She is a writer of poetry, a dancer (guide for JourneyDance) and loves drawing (color crayons are her medium). Find her on Facebook or email her kbuskala@yahoo.com.

Nancy Carlson: I am an evolving poet, writing mostly as reflection, contemplation, gratitude, devotion and as a way of insight into the 'unknown'. I work as an Ayurvedic Health Consultant, Integrative RN, Health/Wellness Coach and teacher, yoga teacher and Reiki Master. You may contact me on Facebook here or my website 'JoyfulHealing' here.

Andreja Cepus is a Social Artist from Slovenia, Europe. After working for several years in the marketing & communications field, she is now fully dedicated to serve through creative communications, hosting and facilitating workshops, spiritual traveling and art inspirational events that are uniting different fields and reawakening the divine feminine principle in our society. www.social-artist.si

Tanielle Childers is a visual artist who thrives on creating vibrant, whimsical artwork with her imagination, intuition and emotions. She also finds great joy and healing in writing short stories and poetry about her life's journey. She and her husband and their two children enjoy life in Loveland, Colorado USA.

Kai Coggin is a poet, teaching artist, and freelancer living on the side of a small mountain in Hot Springs, AR. She holds a degree in Poetry/Creative Writing from Texas A&M University. Her poems focus on love, spirituality, injustice, metaphysics, and beauty. Get PERISCOPE HEART at kaicoggin.com.

Madhava Lata Devi Dasi has been practicing Bhakti Yoga for the past 36 years. Originally from Italy, she now lives in India, where—following a successful career—she continues to study and practice yoga. Her poems are about devotion and are published on her blog 'The Door Ajar to Vraja'. Lately some of her poems have been put to music.

Sarah Courtney Dean is a trans-gender woman and Druid Priestess living in the UK. She has been a poet for as long as she can remember and sees this as part of her role as a Druid Priestess and as a woman. This is a role of encouragement that others, through her, may find a voice.

Louise Marcotte Desrosiers felt spirit calling her to writing in August 2013. Her writing quickly turned to spiritual/inspirational poetry, writing from her heart. In 2014 she recited spoken word at The Holistic Rejuvenation Center in Sacramento, CA. Louise's journey continues through Shamanism, as she follows her soul's calling through healing and writing.

Shailie Dubois has a degree in Psychology. She practices Intuitive Prayer Healing, a combination of her studies in psychology, Christianity, shamanic healing, aromatherapy, artistic expression and a lifetime of dreaming. Her mission is to inspire community rooted in the service of God. She is the writer and illustrator of the children's book *Dani*.

Abra Duprea is a dedicated yoga practitioner who draws inspiration from every facet of this beautiful world. She thrives on nature and love, expressing her creative soul through poetry, photography, and dancing to the beat of her own drum. Follow her journey on Instagram: instagram.com/lonewolfyoga/

Victoria Erickson is based in Austin, TX. Victoria leads creative writing workshops, is a holistic esthetician, massage therapist and Reiki practitioner. To find out more visit her website: victoriaerickson.com, or connect with her on Facebook Victoria Erickson, Writer and Instagram Victoria1031.

Charlotte Eriksson: Originally from Sweden, Charlotte started her own publishing company in London: "Broken Glass Records", through which she released 5 critically acclaimed EPs and 2 full-length albums under the artist name *The Glass Child*. She's authored several books and believes that music can change lives, because it has changed hers. Find her on social media.

Alice Maldonado Gallardo was born in Puerto Rico. She studied Latin American Studies at Mount Holyoke College and then attended Loyola Law School. Alice has worked as an editor, real estate appraiser, translator, secretary, substitute teacher, small business owner and web developer. She lives with her teenage son in Amherst, Massachusetts.

Catherine Ghosh is the creator and Chief Editor of the Journey of the Heart Poetry Project through which she inspires women to release their voices. A practitioner of Bhakti yoga since 1986, she co-founded The Secret Yoga with Graham M. Schweig. Catherine is also an artist, mother, naturalist and free spirit.

Dana Gornall is the co-founder of *The Tattooed Buddha* and mom of three crazy kids and a dog. She has been writing stories since she could put words into sentences, writing books and poems from early on and is still completely in love with language of all kinds. When not working or writing, you can find her lying outside in the dark night gazing up at the millions of stars or dancing in the kitchen with her children.

Salyna Gracie is the Executive Director of the Confluence Gallery and Art Center and a multi-media artist with a focus on dance, poetry and mixed-media collage. Her work explores movement, language and visual symbols that reveal the universal experience…Salyna is a lifelong student of the healing power of art as a deepening spiritual practice and a window into her soul. www.salynagracie.com

Jenn Grosso plays host to the dance of shadow and light, shamelessly wearing her heart on her sleeve while smiling at the fleeting nature of it all. Embracing her inner sacred creative, she focuses on writing, art making, yoga, meditation and picture taking. Connect with Jenn on her blog perilsoftheliving.com

Jennifer Hillman is an artist, published writer/poet with certifications as Intuitive Life Coach/Reiki Master, sharing her services and words on JenniferHillman.com. She supports artists through her radio show. She has two published books of poetry in the series *Embracing Souls: Poetry of the Dance and Words of the Heart.*

Jesse James (Pronouns She/Her or They/Them) At 24, Jesse is a Storyteller & Creatrix of many things; an equal blend of mystical, myth & science. The owner of Artemisian Artes, they use their voice to promote holistic wellness and inclusive activism and advocacy for the many causes they care about.

Jennieke Janaki is from the Netherlands. While traveling the world as a model she found her fulfillment in the practice of yoga, founding 'Sharanam Yoga: Healing Through Surrender' in the Sivananda Lineage. Jennieke authored a poetry book: *Divine Sweetness: Love Aspirations*. She lives every day as an opportunity to realize herself and find the sanctuary within.

Sara Johansson is an intuitive writer, poetess and ascension guide who experienced a spontaneous spiritual awakening in late 2013. With her work and platform, Worlds of Comfort, she is sharing her intuitive gift through the art of healing poetry, words of wisdom, and guidance that is received from the heart of the Sacred Feminine and Divine Mother, for humanity, during these Shifting times. Worldsofcomfrt.com.

Anjuu Kalhaan is a yoga instructor from Delhi, India and mother to one son. Her poems are offerings from her heart. She lives her life practicing gratitude and considers herself to be a very spiritual person.

Jasmine Kang is a writer from California, who also enjoys art, listening to music and being in nature. Her creative work has appeared in various projects. She is also the author of "River of Light", an award-winning collection of prose, poetry and artwork. To know more about Jasmine, visit Moonshinegarden.com

BethAnne Kapansky is a psychologist living in Anchorage, Alaska. She enjoys writing, art, running trails, climbing mountains, chasing rainbows and finding joy in every day with her beloved husband and fur family (aka The Sunshine Crew). She is inspired by nature, beauty, love, books, solitude and chocolate cake.

Kadambari Kashyap is a 21-year old film and music buff and Communications graduate. She enjoys dancing, singing, anchoring shows, making films and directed two films for which she received the Best Ethnographic Film Award at the 4th Bangalore International Short Film Festival, 2014. Currently Kadambari lives in her little hometown in Assam, India.

Krista Katrovas, a yoga teacher and poet, holds a BA in Dance and an MFA in Poetry. Her writing on yoga and women's spirituality has been published in numerous magazines. She has taught yoga in the U.S., Canada and Prague, Czech Republic, she believes in unicorns and loves pizza.

Danielle Kreps is a Plant Spirit Healing Practitioner, Flower Essence Maker, and Teacher in the Kingston, Ontario region. Writing, wildcrafting Flower Essences, and connecting with and singing the Medicine songs of her Plant Spirit Allies are just a few of her passions.

Laura Kutney's love of philosophy and writing started before she can remember. Peeking inside her heart would reveal a whirlwind of feelings surrounding words, books, art, music, photos, beloved people and treasured places. Laura's thoughts, combined with the fact that life is ever-changing, leave her with plenty to write about.

MaRa LuaSa is an Embodiment Mentor & Intuitive Sound Healer. She works with clients worldwide to help empower & awaken those ready to embody their true source self. She fuses a multitude of sacred healing arts-disciplines to support individuals & groups on their unique evolutionary path. Website: MaRaLuaSa.com or CelticHeartHealing.com Email: EmbodyYourSourceLight@gmail.com

Jai Maa is an ordained minister and has been facilitating self-awareness and personal empowerment since 2003 as a Life Coach and Certified Clinical Hypnotherapist. Jai Maa discovered poetry as a healing vehicle and created ThirdEyeSpoken Productions. She is author of "Break Through Your Threshold: A Manual for Faith-Based Manifestation and Co-Creating with God."

Sally MacKinnon is something of a soul surfer of life, diving into experiences that nourish an open heart, playfulness and peace. Her grounding practices personally and professionally are surfing, yoga and meditation and she loves a good run too. Sally writes every day and lives in the mountains and on the beaches of South East Queensland, Australia. www.yourfitnessfriendgc.blogspot.com.au

Darshana Mahtani is a dreamer, a lover, a giver, an optimist, a rebel, a romantic, a breaker of paradigms and stereotypes, and an aspiring novelist. She wants to change the world and find the rest of her tribe. She is part of the {R}evolution happening right now, and you're invited to join.

Taya Malakain has a deep love of poetry as it is the language of the soul. A seeker by nature she has studied World Religions and yoga and meditation for most of her life. She was born, raised and currently lives in Northern California with her son who is a big love and an old soul.

Sara Isabelle Marie is a young woman but an old soul, born and raised in the south of Sweden, on the west coast. She is an author, intuitive writer and a poetess, expressing the heart of the Sacred Feminine and Divine Mother through the art of healing poetry to discover the Inner Sanctum of the Higher Heart, messages of guidance and wisdom that she is receiving intuitively to assist humanity in these incredible, shifting times of Ascension.

Mel Martin is a mother of three, living in Colchester, Essex, U.K, though originally from Dudley in the West Midlands. She has always loved the use of the English language but for many years struggled with basic literacy skills. Everything she achieved in life came through hard work and determination.

Mariann Martland is a writer, a seeker, a lover, a friend. She is a woman finding her voice. Through writing she dances in the dark and breathes in the light. She can be found on Facebook and more of her words can be seen at www.MariannMartland.wordpress.com

Maureen Kwiat Meshenberg relates to poetry as her passion and calling. She writes from the heart and with the purpose of touching and inspiring others on their journey. Maureen published her first volume of poems: "Seasons of the Soul: Transitions and Shifts of Life" and her poetry can be found at the Heart's Calling Poetry Facebook page and blog.

Elizabeth Muccigrosso lives in Gresham, Oregon. She is a full time student and mother of two boys ages 8 and 14 who inspire her to reach her fullest potential. The Phoenix Process also inspires Elizabeth, and she hopes to utilize her life experiences to equally inspire others on this wild and beautiful journey.

Ruth Calder Murphy (Arciemme) is a British writer, artist, musician, wife and mother. She's the author of several published books and several more as yet un-published books. She's passionate about celebrating the uniqueness of people, questioning the unquestionable and discovering new perspectives on old wonders. Find her at ruthcaldermurphy.com

Tracie Nichols is a Contemporary Alchemist, EcoAdvocate, and Teacher who simply can't stop the flood of wordscapes which tumble out, usually at 3 a.m. by the glow of the bathroom nightlight. You can connect with her at TracieNichols.com.

Romana Anna Nova remembers teaching Natural Law throughout many lives since times prehistoric. In this lifetime her main focus is on profound self-initiation and coming back to herself. She's inspiring people to actualize their creative power and become the sole authority in their lives. Connect with her via her website goddessinanna.com

Brigid Clare Oak lives a gentle life of prayer, presence, and poetry; silence and song. She is a lover and communicant with Heaven and Earth, and Their blessed cycles and seasons; beauties, wonders, and inhabitants.

Sonja Phillips-Hollie is a rising poetess, a free spirit, dreamer and spiritualist. She was born in Chicago and now resides in Texas with her husband and three beautiful daughters. Sonja holds a B.A. in Spanish though her life's passion and refuge is poetry. She hopes to inspire women all around the globe to awaken to the inner goddess.

Gwen Potts began her spiritual journey at 21 when she began reading spiritual articles, poetry and books of a spiritual nature. Now at 35 her poetry has become a vehicle of expression and is always written from the depth of her soul. Her poems often well up as a yearning - truly written from the heart. Gwen lives in the UK.

Julia W. Prentice a deeply feeling Cancer, has been writing since her teenage years. The mother of three sons, Julia has successful careers in teaching children, interpretation in sign language and assisting persons with mental health challenges. Living with her love and partner of over forty years has brought contentment and much fulfillment. She writes like she breathes: incessantly!

Zoe Quiney is a writer, poet and dreamer. She calls her heart her home but currently resides in Australia where she admires nature, expresses her heart via words and studies Ayurveda. She is on a constant quest for knowledge, truth and adventure and is passionate about fostering compassion for animals and each other.

Carolyn Riker, M.A. is a teacher, writer and poet in Seattle, WA. She currently writes for several online journals (*Rebelle Society*, *The Tattooed Buddha* and *Elephant Journal*). Her personal blog is (carolynra7.wordpress.com). Carolyn leads journal writing workshops and also offers personal counseling and private tutoring. Additionally, she's completing her first collection of poetry and a children's book.

Carol Reedy Rogero is a 6th grade teacher, late night poet/writer and lover of travel. She scours the beach regularly for trash and heart shaped shells. She blogs at www.thispedestrianlife@wordpress.com, where she hopes readers feel a connection and find something inspirational that speaks to their heart and touches their soul.

Helene Rose's experience provides her with a deeply compassionate perspective and understanding of the modern woman's struggle for mindful living and feminine empowerment. When she writes, she gathers up all the love she feels and experiences and tries to capture it into the words she places on the paper. Find her at helenerose.com.

Marine L. Rot is an award-winning Art Director and a Clarity Coach. Call her a contemporary Muse, who, for the last decade, has been combining her visual talents & emotional intelligence to empower women to awaken to their creative nature and assist them to create a Conscious Life.

Sitara Alaknanda Shakti is a visionary modern-day, mystic medicine woman. She travels from India to Asia, Europe, Indonesia and South America on holy journeys, studying with master shamans and light-workers. Sitara integrates the ancient wisdom of the Indigenous along with the teachings of the stars to awaken the Infinite Love within.

Shivana Sharma has been an educator for the last 33 years and presently serves as the Principal of a Primary School in Trinidad and Tobago. Shivana is a single mother of two beautiful daughters and just finished writing her first children's book. To Shivana, the most joyous sound is that of a child's laughter.

Lisa Smith, at the age of 45, is continuing to discover what makes her tick: mostly a more open, mindful and fun-filled life. She lives in Dorset UK and teaches yoga and mindfulness. Her message to the world is to: 1) Breathe 2) Practice forgiveness, and 3) Be kind to yourself and others.

Rachelle Smith is a poet from Dayton, Ohio. Her poetry is inspired by personal experiences, spirituality and the drive to cause an experience for the reader. The dream to be an author began when she went to Miami University for Creative Writing. Currently, Ms. Smith is finishing her first collection of poetry "Blackberry Wine Blues" to be released the summer of 2015.

Camellia Stadts has been writing for many years but did not fall in love with poetry or creating poetry until recently after going through some of life's earthquakes. Poetry heals her heart and soul. Camellia lives in Detroit and recently graduated with a BA in English from Marygrove College. She has a son, daughter and grandson: her greatest joys. cstadts5215@yahoo.com

Ulli Stanway is an evolving Writer and Poetess. Her life mantra is RIP Pinocchio, your strings have served you well and now it is time to cut you loose, so you can skip down your own path. Barefoot, if you wish. You can connect with Ulli via her blog www.desireyourownhappiness.com.

Tammy T. Stone is a Canadian writer, photographer and wellness practitioner currently living in Japan. Her poetry, articles and short stories have appeared in numerous literary publications internationally. She has recently published her first poetry collection inspired by her travels, "Formation: Along the Ganges and Back Again" with Prolific Press. Visit her website: tammystonewrites.wordpress.com

Savitri Talahatu holds an E-RYT500, is an inter-disciplinary teacher who has taught in the public system in Canada and Indonesia. Savitri is a yoga and meditation educator, lifestyle coach, holistic health practitioner, doula, and Reiki Master. She is passionate about inspiring others to make healthy lifestyle choices and empowering them to find gateways to wholeness.

Taruni Devi Dasi Tan is a Music therapist, grief counselor and co-founder of three tech startups. Currently residing in New York, she dedicates her spare time to running free community grief support groups, mentoring young adults interested in a more spiritual, heart centered approach to life and volunteering at hospice.

Nirvani Teasley is a veteran Navy wife, mother of four grown children and two adorable granddaughters. She is a long time folk art painter and fabric artist. In the last two years, she has evolved from her lifelong passion for reading poetry, to writing it. She loves penning poems that emphasize the Divine Feminine.

Rosemerry Wahtola Trommer's poetry has appeared in *O Magazine*, in back alleys, on A Prairie Home Companion and on river rocks. She was recently appointed Poet Laureate of Colorado's Western Slope. Since 2005, she's written a poem a day. Favorite one-word mantra: *Adjust*.

Kathi Valeii is a reproductive justice and birth advocate living in Michigan. She writes about the full spectrum of reproductive health issues at her blog, birthanarchy.com Poetry has been a form of self-soothing ever since she tumbled into it following her divorce. She and her partner parent three children together.

Jackie VanCampen is author of *Letters to my Daughter: A Mother's Journey of Healing and Transformation*. She is a "Wise Heart Writer," which means that she writes wisdoms of the heart. When Jackie writes she feels as if she's connecting with the essence of who I am, named Kahlia. Her writings speak to the Divine Feminine Goddess in each woman.

Lynda Grace Vargas is a retired foreign language and elementary school teacher who loves Romance languages and opera. She lives in San Diego with her husband of nearly fifty years where they enjoy a vegetarian lifestyle, watching hummingbirds, and catching their Tuxedo cat Sox, in one adorable position after another.

Alise Versella is a 24 year old poet from the Jersey Shore. Always one to find beauty in the pain, Alise writes to show others they are not alone in their heartaches and that poetry is a beautiful salve to heal our deepest wounds. You can visit her at her website www.aliseversella.net

Bryonie Wise is an alchemist of the heart & believes that when we come from a place of love, anything is possible. When not teaching yoga or writing her heart to the bones, she can be found frolicking in the sunshine with her camera & her dog, Winston, living her yoga.

Eva Xanthopoulos is a Greco-American writer, artist, and life-coach. She received her B.A. in Creative Writing from Cleveland State University. Her works are published online and in-print (*Golden Lantern, Mystic Living Today, Boston Magazine, Journey Magazine,* etc.) Eva is the Founder of Poehemian Press and the Co-Founder of Etheric Archives.

Dominique Youkhehpaz is the founder of Self-Marriage Ceremonies, a pathway of marrying yourself, marrying Spirit and committing to what matters most. She is also a dedicated student of the Awakening Women Institute, a practice of embodied feminine spirituality. To find out more about her two loves, go to selfmarriageceremonies.com and awakeningwomen.com

Jennifer Courtney Zechlin is a poet, artist, mother, grandmother, daughter, friend and soon-to-be wife. Jennifer is an American and is working on becoming a Brit. "There are so many I AMs that I am and I AMs I will become someday. Through it all, I have been a lover of life."

About the Artists

Julia Pankratova first introduced me to her beautiful artwork two years ago when she first came upon the poetry project online. A Russian artist who had relocated to New Jersey in 1999, Julia found inspiration in the work of the Journey of the Heart poets. Having explored intuitive mandala art for her own personal healing and transformation in 2009, Julia took wholeheartedly to the practice, for some time, creating one mandala a day.

Mandala is a Sanskrit word meaning "circle," or "round." Mandalas are rich, primal symbols that shed light on the deepest levels of our consciousness. The archetypal force embedded in the perfect geometry of a circle connects the human psyche with its own innate harmony. Circles are sacred spaces, the shape of the cosmos, openings that welcome us in. Soft, curvy and enveloping, the Divine Feminine is represented emblematically with a circle. Characterized by interiority, interconnectivity, and fullness of being, circles foster mutual respect and cooperation. They are symbols of peace and communication.

As the symbolism in mandalas resonated so beautifully with the spirit of our poetry project, I invited Julia to custom create mandalas for each of the book's chapter themes. Informed by her intuitive training, she drew thirteen ink mandalas for us by hand. Much like the poetry in this book, her creations flowed freely from her heart and spirit. Without the use of any instruments the mandalas' carefree imprecision seem to highlight a unique beauty that reflects the unique voices behind the poetry.

Shailie Dubois, our cover artist, also practices intuitive healing. As a regular contributor of poetry to our project, Shailie was spontaneously moved to create a beautiful cover for our book. Independently of Julia, Shailie's intuitive art practice also led her to paint Mandalas!

Shailie's artwork glows with the joy, the wonder and magic the women in this project generated together. She gives us faces and therefore personhood, hinting at the intimate sharing we have to offer, and diverse backgrounds we come from. And she paints us in a circle, like a single organism, sharing a heartbeat.

On the front cover Shailie gently scatters us like stars across a mystical universe, and then plants us like flowers in the meadow of spring colors on the back cover. Her generous and playful strokes capture the range of voices found in the book, and the expansive journeys we take through our poetry.

Acknowledgments

This book was birthed through the combined vision and effort of over 80 women from the Journey of the Heart Poetry Project. Although the beautiful energy of each of these women nourished this project as it grew, there are a few very inspired sisters who really poured their hearts into the production of this book, and whose dedicated efforts really fueled its production. Here we recognize each of them with gratitude for their individual contributions.

Firstly, many thanks to our initial team of 28 volunteers who oversaw and encouraged the book's production at various stages of development: Charu Agarwal, Sandra Allagapen, Milly Bozovic, Ginny Brannan, Yvonne Brewer, Anita Grace Brown, Jamie Burgess, Kim Buskala, Andreja Cepus, Kai Coggin, Nancy Carlson, Shailie Dubois, Jenn Grosso, Jesse James, Jasmine Kang, Sally Mackinnon, Alice Maldonado Gallardo, Mariann Martland, Maureen Kwiat Meshenberg, Ruth Calder Murphy, Tracie Nichols, Julia Prentice, Carolyn Riker, Camellia Stadts, Tammy Stone, Savitri Talahatu and Alise Versella. Over the months of book production we became like a sisterhood working closely with each other to achieve our vision.

An extra special thanks to a handful of dedicated sisters who had the arduous task of sensitivity sorting through over 400 submissions and selecting the 169 poems that appear in this book. Sandra, Tammy, Jamie and Shailie: your diligence, and the delicate care with which you handled everyone's poems—ever intent on not excluding anyone's voice—is much appreciated. This core group of sisters would like to especially thank Sandra for collating all the poems into chapter documents for easy reference, and to Tracie, Carolyn, Sally, Nancy and Kim who helped fine-tune the distribution of poems into chapter themes.

Much appreciation to all of our proofreaders: Julie, Jamie, Carolyn, Savitri, Tammy, Camellia, Sally and Jesse, whose gentle editing of the poetry took every comma and semicolon into consideration when handing out literary allowances, so was not to stifle the full expression of the individual poets.

Our heartfelt gratitude to the lovely Shailie Dubois, who hand-painted our beautiful and original cover art, as well as created our book's promotional trailer. Thank you also to intuitive Russian artist, Julia Pankratova, who drew the delightful pen and ink mandalas adorning each of our chapters, in accordance with their themes.

Thanks to Camellia for her inspired idea to create T-shirts for the project, to Jamie for her research toward achieving this, and to her husband Jason for kindly creating the graphic transparency required for the artwork.

This book, as we know it, would have not been possible without the generous efforts of our kind sister, fellow poet and publisher, Alice of Golden Dragonfly Press, whose positive attitude has encouraged this project from beginning to end. Alice is responsible for reading through the hundreds of poems submitted to the project this year and organizing them by themes, designing the book's cover, designing the book's interior structure, formatting our book as an e-book, promoting the book, etc.

Lastly, we extend our most loving appreciations to each and every one of you who opened up your hearts, made yourself vulnerable and shared such intimate poetry with all of us. Thank you for trusting us with your wise and wild, gentle yet strong, sweet and insightful, most valuable voices. It is on the foundation of your courage and inspiration that the Journey of the Heart Women's Spiritual Poetry Project was built.

May we each continue energizing and supporting one another, and all sisters that cross our paths in life, in honor of the spiritual energy that connects us all and the beautiful and unique ways that it emerges through our voices, our poetry.

Made in the USA
San Bernardino, CA
01 August 2015